Financial Literacy
Lessons & Activities

Grade 2

Writing: Leslie Barnard Booth
Content Editing: Kathleen Jorgensen
Lisa Vitarisi Mathews
Copy Editing: Laurie Westrich
Art Direction: Yuki Meyer
Cover Design: Yuki Meyer
Illustration: Robin Boyer
Design/Production: Paula Acojido
Jessica Onken

EMC 3122

Visit
teaching-standards.com
to view a correlation
of this book.

**Correlated to
Current Standards**

**Congratulations on your purchase of some of the
finest teaching materials in the world.**

*Photocopying the pages in this book
is permitted for <u>single-classroom use only</u>.
Making photocopies for additional classes
or schools is prohibited.*

For information about other Evan-Moor products, call 1-800-777-4362,
fax 1-800-777-4332, or visit our website, www.evan-moor.com.
Entire contents © 2022 Evan-Moor Corporation
10 Harris Court, Suite C-3, Monterey, CA 93940-5773. Printed in USA.

CPSIA: Sheridan Saline, Inc., Saline, MI, USA [9/2023]

Why Teach Financial Literacy?

Preparing students to understand financial concepts in school and in the real world includes teaching them about money and giving them the information that they need to be informed consumers. The foundational concepts of earning, buying, saving, and borrowing can be taught at the earliest grade levels, when children start developing habits with money. The concepts of investing and protecting money can be introduced a few years later.

For many people, transactions frequently happen electronically through tap-and-go technology in stores, online shopping, and electronic funds transfers to pay bills. Some children may rarely see actual money changing hands. This may mean that they have less opportunity to connect money's value to the things it buys. Handling bills and coins, even if they are play money, gives children a concrete understanding of how we use money to get other things of value.

Having information about how the financial world works helps people make appropriate decisions for themselves to meet their own needs and goals. Young adults need to be prepared before stepping fully into an adult's world, where there are so many risks for making mistakes with money. While people's choices are personal and may vary widely from one person to the next, everyone must find a way to navigate through a variety of financial structures.

As you present financial concepts to students, consider their diverse backgrounds and their varying world views, encouraging them to form their own opinions and share their ideas about spending, saving, credit, and more. As students grow and change, their approach to financial literacy concepts and skills may also change. It is important to provide them the tools they need so they can make the best decisions for themselves and to empower them with a solid foundation to become informed consumers who have their own financial identities.

Contents

Units

Financial Concepts: The value of a good or service is what you would trade for it.
Money acts as a standard measure of value to make trading easy.
Trading (buying and selling) involves cooperative exchanges.

Math Skills: skip counting, addition, subtraction, currency

Financial Concepts: While we need some foods and items to live, other foods and items are wants.
Shoppers need to prioritize what is most important, especially if money is limited.

Math Skills: skip counting, addition, subtraction, currency

Financial Concepts: Decisions made about clothing involve many features that can be ranked.
Clothing purchases need to fit the purpose and the wearer.

Math Skills: skip counting, addition, subtraction, currency

Financial Concepts: Money from gifts or chores provides valuable experience in spending.
Spending money develops a sense of items' worth and value.
Money earned for chores helps connect responsibility and effort to earning.

Math Skills: skip counting, addition, subtraction, currency

Financial Literacy Lessons and Activities • EMC 3122 • © Evan-Moor Corporation

Financial Literacy Lessons and Activities lets students get hands-on with personal finance. Based on national standards from the Council for Economic Education and the Jump$tart Coalition, these lessons and activities make using money concrete for students in real-life situations.

10 Engaging Units

Financial Literacy Lessons and Activities offers 10 units on grade-level topics involving the use of money. Each unit's topic focuses on a place where money is spent, things that money is spent on, or ways to receive money. The units bring together vocabulary and financial concepts using a story and explicit instruction. Practice includes math application problems and an engaging activity.

Unit Features

Units are designed to fit into a weekly lesson plan. Each 12-page unit provides information for the teacher, a story, vocabulary, concept practice, math application, and an activity.

Teacher Overview

An introduction telling what students may and may not be familiar with in the unit topic

A suggested plan for using each part of the unit

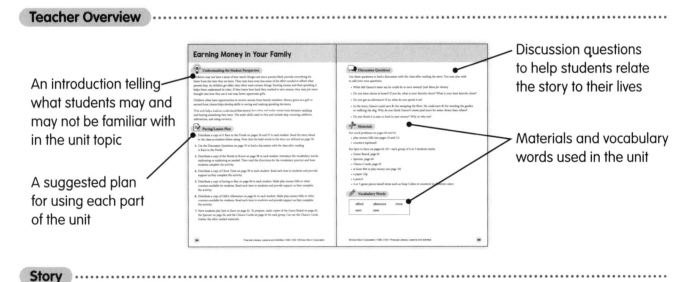

Discussion questions to help students relate the story to their lives

Materials and vocabulary words used in the unit

Story

A two-page story that introduces the topic in context, as well as the vocabulary that students will learn

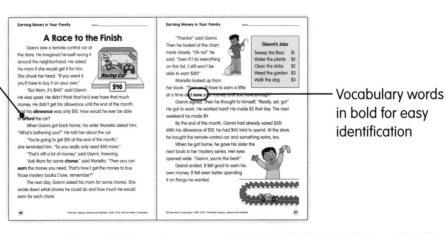

Vocabulary words in bold for easy identification

Vocabulary and Concept Practice ··

Definitions and practice writing the words in context sentences

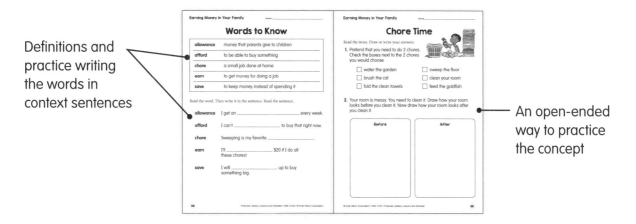

An open-ended way to practice the concept

Math Application ···

Scenarios using money-based word problems; manipulatives and other aids provided

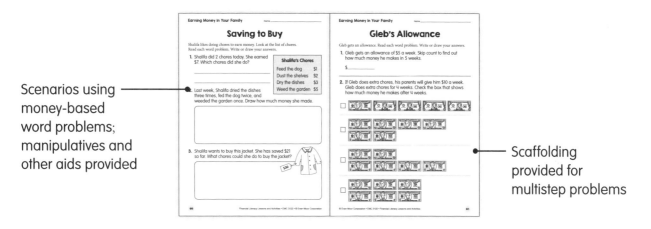

Scaffolding provided for multistep problems

Activity ···

A fun art activity, game, role-play, or other activity that lets students practice using money in the unit's context

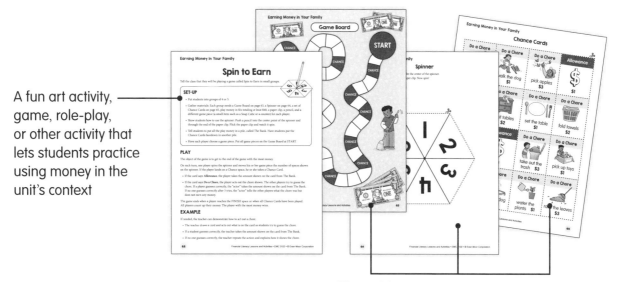

Cutouts, fill-in tables, and game boards provided

Cutouts, reference sheets, and other aids support student learning through all units:

Play money dollar bills to use as manipulatives and in games

Play money coins and higher bills to use as manipulatives

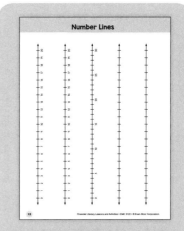

Number lines to support skip counting and repeated adding

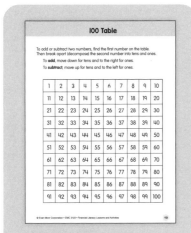

100 table to help with adding and subtracting tens and ones

Money place-value mat for sorting coins, adding, and subtracting

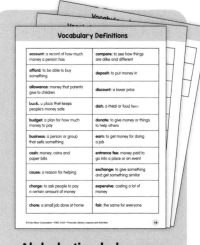

Alphabetized glossary of all vocabulary words in the book

Answer Key

Provided for the Math Application pages. The correct answer or a description of an acceptable response is shown.

How to Use *Financial Literacy Lessons and Activities*

Support for Consumers-to-Be

Encourage students to relate the concepts and experiences they read about to their own lives. Be mindful not to judge their choices or habits and to respect cultural and family attitudes toward using money. Tell them how money works, not how they should or shouldn't use it.

Key Words

As you decide which, if not all, of the pages in each unit you will print out for your students, be sure to include the Words to Know page that defines key concept terms. This page is useful throughout the unit. Have students tape it to their desks for easy reference. If you send a page home for homework, send the Words to Know page, as well, for support.

The Importance of Discussion

There is no one right way to earn, spend, or save money. Facilitate student discussions so that they can share ideas, thoughts, and habits. Learning from others' successes and struggles improves planning and problem-solving skills.

Connections to Other Subjects

The units in this book provide opportunities to describe characters, identify sequence and cause and effect, and increase vocabulary (reading/language arts). The units augment learning about different people's needs and wants, how a community works together, and taking responsibility (social studies). The word problems let students practice handling money, basic arithmetic, and reasoning (math).

Keeping It Playful

Use play money frequently. Consider having a good supply of play money ready before starting to use the book and collecting it after each lesson to use throughout the year. The activities at the ends of the units provide opportunities for students to work together, use hands-on materials, make decisions for themselves, and often create something meaningful.

For Non-U.S. Classrooms

While this book uses U.S. coins and bills, it can be used in any country. If your country's main denomination is not the dollar, substitute *euro, yuan, pound, rupee, riyal,* or whatever is appropriate along with your equivalent of *cent*. Practicing one-to-many correspondence is still useful for students, as are the decision-making and reasoning challenges provided.

Financial Literacy Lessons and Activities • EMC 3122 • © Evan-Moor Corporation

Play Money Cutouts: coins, $5s, $10s, $20s

Number Lines

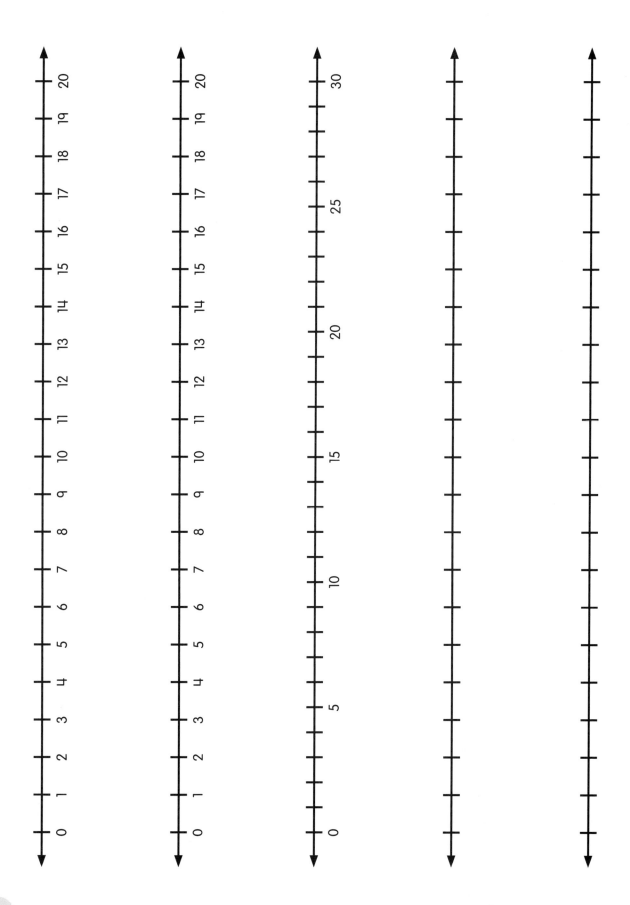

Financial Literacy Lessons and Activities • EMC 3122 • © Evan-Moor Corporation

100 Table

To add or subtract two numbers, find the first number on the table.
Then break apart (decompose) the second number into tens and ones.

To **add**, move down for tens and to the right for ones.

To **subtract**, move up for tens and to the left for ones.

1	2	3	4	5	6	7	8	9	10
11	12	13	14	15	16	17	18	19	20
21	22	23	24	25	26	27	28	29	30
31	32	33	34	35	36	37	38	39	40
41	42	43	44	45	46	47	48	49	50
51	52	53	54	55	56	57	58	59	60
61	62	63	64	65	66	67	68	69	70
71	72	73	74	75	76	77	78	79	80
81	82	83	84	85	86	87	88	89	90
91	92	93	94	95	96	97	98	99	100

Money Place-Value Mat

Dollars (100s)	Dimes (10s)	Pennies (1s)

Financial Literacy Lessons and Activities • EMC 3122 • © Evan-Moor Corporation

Vocabulary Definitions

account: a record of how much money a person has	**compare:** to see how things are alike and different
afford: to be able to buy something	**deposit:** to put money in
allowance: money that parents give to children	**discount:** a lower price
bank: a place that keeps people's money safe	**dish:** a meal or food item
budget: a plan for how much money to pay	**donate:** to give money or things to help others
business: a person or group that sells something	**earn:** to get money for doing a job
cash: money; coins and paper bills	**entrance fee:** money paid to go into a place or an event
cause: a reason for helping	**exchange:** to give something and get something similar
charge: to ask people to pay a certain amount of money	**expensive:** costing a lot of money
chore: a small job done at home	**fair:** the same for everyone

Vocabulary Definitions, *continued*

fare: money that someone pays to ride	**need:** must have or do something
feature: an important part of something	**order:** to ask for something you want to eat
flier: a sheet that tells about an event or an item	**package:** an item sent to someone in a box
food bank: a place that collects food for people who need it	**pass:** a card or paper that lets you enter
fundraiser: a way to collect money for something	**passenger:** someone who rides a bus, train, plane, or boat
future: a time that hasn't happened yet	**price:** how much you have to pay for something
goal: something you want to do or have	**price tag:** a label that shows how much something costs
host: a person who seats people at a restaurant	**sale:** a time when prices are lower
mail: to send something through the post office	**save:** to keep money instead of spending it
menu: a list of choices	**savings:** money that someone has saved

Financial Literacy Lessons and Activities • EMC 3122 • © Evan-Moor Corporation

server: a person who helps people at a restaurant	**want:** to wish for something
shipping: moving something to another place	**weigh:** to find out how heavy something is
spend: to pay money to buy something	**withdraw:** to take money out
stamp: a sticker that shows how much you paid	
teller: a person who helps customers at a bank	
tip: money to give to a helpful person	
total: the amount of everything added together	
trade: to give something and get something different	
travel: to go to another place	
wallet: a holder for money that folds	

Using Money to Trade

Understanding the Student Perspective

Children start trading things with each other at a young age: they see a sibling or a friend with something that they want, and they offer something in return. Ever since coins came into use 5,000 years ago, traders have been able to exchange goods and services for something of universal value: money.

By the time children are in school, they realize that they can't have everything they want, and that others may want similar things. Fairness is important to them. However, they must remember that both people must agree that a trade is fair.

This unit helps students understand that trading involves giving and receiving goods or services that are worth about the same. They can use money in the trade, and both traders should get something they want. The math skills used in this unit include skip counting, addition, subtraction, and using currency.

Pacing/Lesson Plan

1. Distribute a copy of The Newspaper Business on pages 20 and 21 to each student. Read the story aloud to the class as students follow along. Note that the bold words in the story are defined on page 22.

2. Use the Discussion Questions on page 19 to lead a discussion with the class after reading The Newspaper Business.

3. Distribute a copy of the Words to Know on page 22 to each student. Introduce the vocabulary words, rephrasing or explaining as needed. Then read the directions for the vocabulary practice and have students complete the activity.

4. Distribute a copy of This for That on page 23 to each student. Read each item to students and provide support as they complete the activity.

5. Distribute a copy of Alondra's Bracelets on page 24 to each student. Make play-money bills or other counters available for students. Read each item to students and provide support as they complete the activity.

6. Distribute a copy of Buying and Trading on page 25 to each student. Make play-money coins or other counters available for students. Read each item to students and provide support as they complete the activity.

7. Have students do the Class Gift-Swap Party activity on page 26. To prepare, make copies of the Gift Cards on pages 27–29 and cut them out. Make sure there is one card per player. Also provide enough play money for the activity.

Discussion Questions

Use these questions to lead a discussion with the class after reading the story. You may also wish to add your own questions.

- In the story, what did the children trade a copy of their newspaper for? *[a picture]*
  Do you think that this was a fair trade? Why or why not?

- Have you ever traded with someone? If so, what things did you trade?

- Think of a special thing that belongs to you such as a fun toy, a favorite shirt, or a soccer ball. Would you trade it for anything? If so, what?

- In the story, Daniella said the newspaper should be 10 cents because it is a short newspaper. Do you think a short newspaper should cost less than a long newspaper? Why or why not?

 Materials

For word problems on pages 24 and 25:
- play-money coins and bills (see pages 10 and 11)
- counters (optional)

For Class Gift-Swap Party on pages 26–29—each student needs:
- one Gift Card from pages 27–29
- $15 in play money (see page 10)

 Vocabulary Words

business	exchange	fair
price	trade	

Name _____

The Newspaper Business

It was writing time at school. Daniella and her friends Mikey and Hyejung got an idea. They want to make a newspaper. It will tell about things that happen at school.

The three friends worked on the words and pictures. They wrote about the games they played in gym class. Mikey made a picture of a classmate kicking a ball really far. They wrote about what they learned in their math lesson, but they couldn't think of a picture for it. Daniella said, "Let's **exchange** it for a story about our science lesson." They used a drawing from their science journal.

When they were all done, Daniella said, "Hey! We could sell this newspaper to people!"

"Yeah!" said Hyejung. "We could have our own **business**!"

"What **price** should we sell one newspaper for?" asked Mikey.

"We should get 1 dollar," said Hyejung.

"It's a short newspaper," said Daniella, "so maybe 10 cents."

"How about 25 cents?" suggested Mikey.

"That's a good price," agreed Hyejung and Daniella.

Their teacher made copies of the newspaper.

After school, some kids stayed to play. Parents were standing around talking. Daniella, Mikey, and Hyejung told people about the newspaper.

Mikey's mom bought a copy of the newspaper. Hyejung's dad did, too. A girl named Sophia also wanted to buy a copy. But she didn't have any money.

"Could I **trade** something for it instead?" asked Sophia.

Daniella thought about it. A trade would be good as long as it was **fair**. "What do you want to trade for it?"

Sophia held out a picture she had made in art class.

"Oooooh! I love it," said Hyejung.

"Me, too," said Mikey. They made the trade.

Later, Daniella, Mikey, and Hyejung were walking home from school. Daniella was holding Sophia's picture. "You know what would make our newspaper business even better?" said Daniella.

"What?" asked Hyejung.

"If Sophia joined our business and made art for our newspaper!"

"Yes!" said Mikey and Hyejung at the same time.

"Let's ask her to join us tomorrow!" said Daniella.

Words to Know

exchange	to give something and get something similar
business	a person or group that sells something
price	how much you have to pay for something
trade	to give something and get something different
fair	the same for everyone

Read the word. Then write it in the sentence. Read the sentence.

exchange I will _____ this shirt for a bigger one.

business I am starting a babysitting _____.

price The _____ for this bike is too high.

trade I want to _____ my crayons for candy.

fair Let's take turns so it is _____.

Name _____

This for That

Read the items. Draw or write your answers.
There are no right or wrong answers.

1. Look at the trades below. Circle the one that seems the most fair.

a bike  for a crayon

_____

a camera  for a skateboard

_____

a cake  for a book

2. My brother wants my new toy car. He will trade me 3 of his older toy cars for my new one. Do you think this is a fair trade? Tell why or why not.

_____

_____

_____

Name _____

Alondra's Bracelets

Read about how Alondra makes money.
Write or draw your answers.

Alondra makes bracelets and sells them.
People trade money for the bracelets.

1. In the morning, Alondra sold 4 bracelets
for $2 each. Skip count to figure out how
much money she earned.

$ _____

2. In the afternoon, Alondra earned $6.
Draw how many bracelets she sold.

3. How much money did Alondra make in all?

$ _____

Name _____

Buying and Trading

Read each word problem. Write or draw your answers.

1. Henri bought a bouncy ball from Samir. He traded all the coins below for the ball. How much did Henri pay for it?

_____ ¢

2. Samir went to the candy store with the money he got from Henri. The peppermints cost 10¢ each. He bought 5 peppermints. Skip count to figure out how much he paid.

_____ ¢

3. How much money does Samir have left over?

_____ ¢

Class Gift-Swap Party

Tell the class to pretend that they are having a party, and each student will receive a pretend gift. They will each get a card showing their pretend gift. They will have a chance to trade for a different gift.

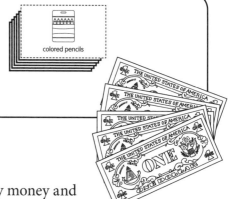

WHAT YOU NEED

- Gift Cards on pages 27–29

- play money in $1s

WHAT YOU DO

Put students in groups of about 8 players, sitting in a circle. Give $5 of play money and one Gift Card to each player.

Have players look at their card. One at a time, have each player tell his or her group what gift he or she has.

On each turn, the player says either "I'll keep my gift" or "I want to trade my gift for another" and states which one. The owner of the other gift says "yes," "no," or "I'll trade for money."

- If "yes," the players trade Gift Cards, and it is the next player's turn.

- If "no," the players keep their Gift Cards, and it is the next player's turn.

- If "I'll trade for money," the players discuss a price. If they agree on a price, they trade money for the Gift Card. The first player keeps both Gift Cards.

Play continues until all players are happy with what they have or until a time limit set by the teacher has been reached.

EXAMPLE

If needed, the teacher can demonstrate play with a student similar to the following:

Teacher:	I want to trade my jump rope for the sled.
Player with sled:	I'll trade for money.
Teacher:	Okay, I'll give you $3.
Player:	I want $4.
Teacher:	It's a deal! *(Player gives teacher the Gift Card, teacher gives player $4)*

Gift Cards

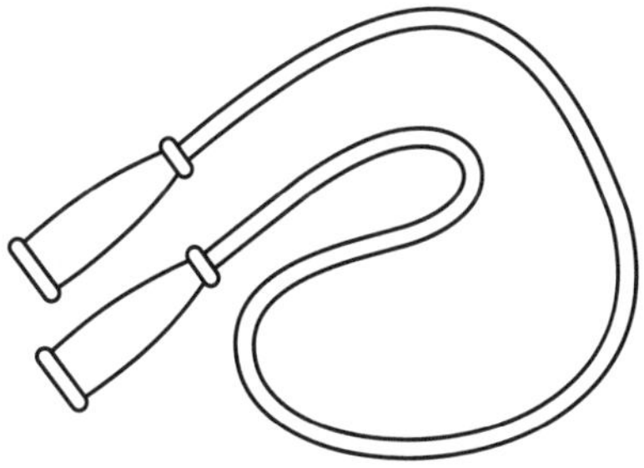

jump rope

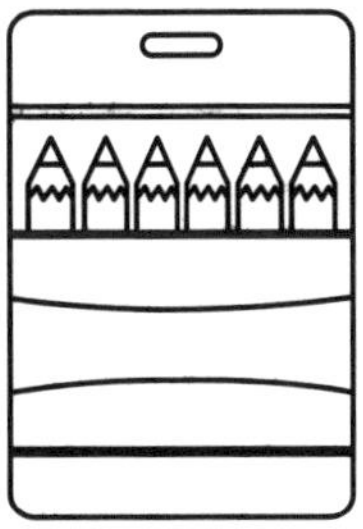

colored pencils

beading kit

sled

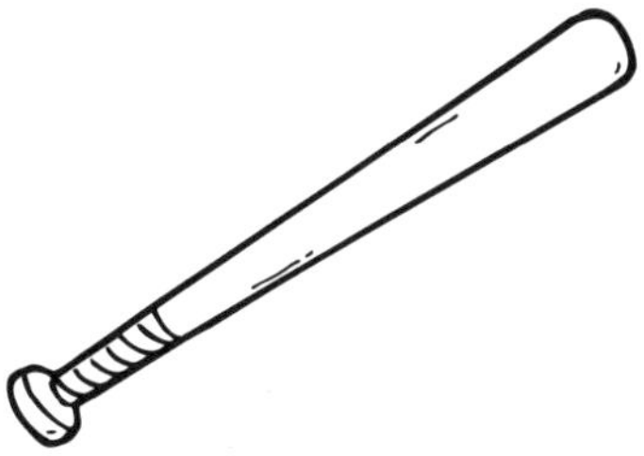

bat

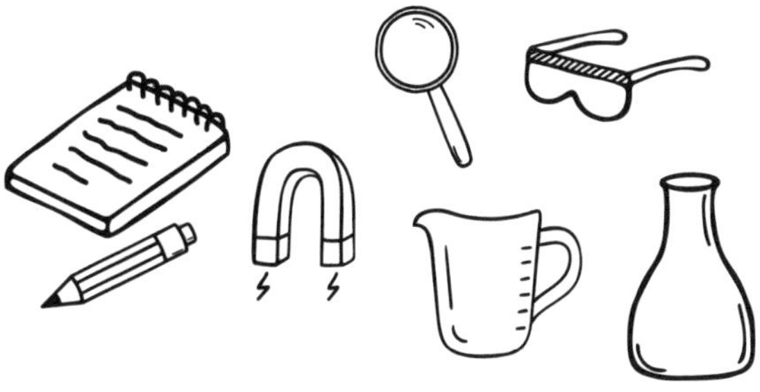

science kit

skateboard

toy car

Gift Cards

doll

paint set

board game

toy robot

roller skates

clay set

toy rocket

toy cat

Gift Cards

book

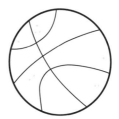

basketball

toy unicorn

maracas

guitar

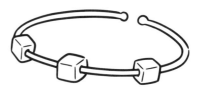

bracelet

action figure

camera

Buying Groceries

 Understanding the Student Perspective

Children often go to the grocery store with their parents. Some people write a list before they go to the store. The list may have things they need and things they want. Some people may be able to buy only what they need; they may not have enough money to buy everything they want. This is a concept that is often difficult for children to understand. Learning about how much money different goods cost may help make this concept more meaningful to children.

This unit helps students understand that people have to make choices about what to buy. These choices sometimes depend on how much money they have available to spend. The math skills used in this unit include skip counting, addition, subtraction, and using currency.

 Pacing/Lesson Plan

1. Distribute a copy of Grocery Shopping Helper on pages 32 and 33 to each student. Read the story aloud to the class as students follow along. Note that the bold words in the story are defined on page 34.

2. Use the Discussion Questions on page 31 to lead a discussion with the class after reading Grocery Shopping Helper.

3. Distribute a copy of the Words to Know on page 34 to each student. Introduce the vocabulary words, rephrasing or explaining as needed. Then read the directions for the vocabulary practice and have students complete the activity.

4. Distribute a copy of Needs and Wants on page 35 to each student. Read each item to students and provide support as they complete the activity.

5. Distribute a copy of Akash's Cupcakes on page 36 to each student. Make play-money bills or other counters available for students. Read each item to students and provide support as they complete the activity.

6. Distribute a copy of Jayleen's Apple Problem on page 37 to each student. Make play-money coins and bills or other counters available for students. Read each item to students and provide support as they complete the activity.

7. Have students do the Let's Shop for a Picnic activity on page 38. To prepare, make copies of the Picnic Foods on page 39, the Shopping List on page 40, and Our Picnic Blanket on page 41. Gather the other needed materials.

Discussion Questions

Use these questions to lead a discussion with the class after reading the story. You may also wish to add your own questions.

- Have you ever helped buy groceries? If so, what was it like?

- In the story, Dad had a list of everything he needed. What do you think might happen if he didn't have a list?

- In the story, the different types of bread had different prices. Why do you think some types of bread cost more than other types?

- Have you ever compared the prices of two or more items at a store? Tell about it.

 Materials

For word problems on pages 36 and 37:
- play-money coins and bills (see pages 10 and 11)
- counters (optional)

For Let's Shop for a Picnic on pages 38–41—each pair of students needs:
- Picnic Foods, page 39
- Shopping List, page 40
- Our Picnic Blanket, page 41
- $25 in play money for each student (see pages 10 and 11)
- pencils
- crayons
- scissors
- glue or tape

 Vocabulary Words

budget	compare	need
spend	total	want

Grocery Shopping Helper

Today Crystal was helping her dad shop for groceries. "We have a **budget** of $25," Dad said. "That means we have $25 to **spend** today, and we can't spend more than that."

"What's on our list?" asked Crystal.

Dad showed her the list. "This is all stuff we **need** for dinner tonight and breakfast tomorrow," he said.

They walked down the first row of items. Crystal saw the bread. She pulled the first loaf she saw off the shelf.

"Wait," said Dad. "That kind costs a lot. Every kind has a different price." He pointed to the prices on the shelf. "Let's **compare** each kind to see which one is best for us."

Grocery List
pasta
pasta sauce
bread
milk
apples
carrots
lettuce

They looked at all the different kinds of bread. There was white, wheat, rye, and pumpernickel! Some had seeds on the crust. The loaves were different, too. There were long loaves and round loaves, big and small. So many choices! "Can we get whole wheat? I like it the best," said Crystal. She found a loaf of whole wheat bread with a lower price. "Let's get this kind instead," she said.

They put the bread in their cart. Then they walked past the chocolate bars. "I **want** one of those!" said Crystal.

"Me, too," said Dad, "but they're not on our list. It's important to get everything on our list first. There might not be enough money left over for other things."

"Okay," said Crystal. They kept looking for the items on their list. Soon they had found them all.

"Good work!" said Dad. "We found everything!" Then he started adding up the prices of all the items in their cart. He said the numbers out loud as he added. "Three plus six is nine, nine plus two…"

"Why are you doing math?" asked Crystal.

"I want to know the **total** of everything in our cart. Let's make sure that it won't cost more than our budget," Dad explained.

He finished adding. "We did it!"

"Really?" asked Crystal.

"Yes," said Dad. "Our budget is $25, but these things cost $23 total. That leaves $2 extra! You can pick out anything you want, as long as it costs $2 or less."

"Hooray!" said Crystal. She chose a chocolate bar. They paid for their groceries and carried them to the car. Then Dad pulled out the chocolate bar and gave it to Crystal. She broke it in two and gave half to her dad.

"Thank you! You sure are a great grocery shopping helper!" said Dad.

Name _____

Words to Know

budget	a plan for how much money to pay
spend	to pay money to buy something
need	must have or do something
compare	to see how things are alike and different
want	to wish for something
total	the amount of everything added together

Read the word. Then write it in the sentence. Read the sentence.

budget The class _____ for art supplies is $50.

spend He will _____ his extra money on toys.

need We _____ chicken for dinner tonight.

compare Let's _____ the prices of these pencils.

want I really _____ these rainbow socks.

total The books cost a _____ of $9.

Name _____

Needs and Wants

Read the items. Draw or write your answers.

1. Pretend that you are planning breakfast for your family. Make a list of some food items that you **need**.

Breakfast List

_____

_____

_____

_____

_____

_____

2. Now think of a food that you **want** to buy at the grocery store. Draw it in the box.

Name _____

Akash's Cupcakes

Akash wants to make cupcakes for his family. Read about his shopping trip. Write or draw your answers.

1. To make cupcakes, Akash needs to buy all the items below. Look at the prices of the items. How much money does Akash need in all?

$ _____

---

2. Look at the money that Akash brought. Does he have enough money to buy everything he needs?

yes   **no**

---

3. How much more money does Akash need?

$ _____

Name _____

Jayleen's Apple Problem

Jayleen is shopping with her mom.
Read each word problem.
Write or draw your answers.

Red Apples
50¢ each

Green Apples
25¢ each

1. Jayleen's mom asks her to choose 4 apples.
If Jayleen chooses 4 red apples, how much will they cost in all?

50¢   50¢   50¢   50¢

$_____

2. If Jayleen chooses 4 green apples, how much will they cost in all?

25¢   25¢   25¢   25¢

$_____

3. If Jayleen chooses the red apples instead of the green apples,
how much more money will she spend?

$_____

Let's Shop for a Picnic

Tell the class that they will pretend to go grocery shopping with a partner.
They have $25 to buy food for a picnic.

WHAT YOU NEED

- Picnic Foods, page 39, one per pair
- Shopping List, page 40, one per pair
- Our Picnic Blanket, page 41, one per pair
- play money (five $1s, two $5s, and one $10) per pair
- pencils
- scissors
- crayons
- glue or tape

WHAT YOU DO

1. Put students in pairs. Give each pair of students a copy of the Picnic Foods and the Shopping List, along with $25 in play money. Tell students they are going shopping for a picnic. The pair's budget is $25.

2. Tell students to look at the Picnic Foods and choose the foods they want for their picnic. Tell them to write those foods on their Shopping List, along with the price of each food they chose. They do not have to fill the list.

3. Next, have students add up all the prices of the items on their list. Remind them that their budget is $25. If their items add up to more than $25, they need to change their list or take some items off.

4. When their lists are ready, they pay you, the cashier, for their foods.

5. Have students color the foods they bought on the Picnic Foods sheet, cut them out, and attach them to the blanket on the Our Picnic Blanket page.

Picnic Foods

noodles $3	nuts $6	pizza $5	potato salad $4
tortillas $4	beans $3	ham $5	tofu $5
cheese $6	crackers $5	chips $4	dip $5
watermelon $4	apples $3	cherries $4	grapes $4
doughnuts $6	pie $7	cookies $4	cake $9

Name _____

Name _____

Shopping List

Item	Price
	$
	$
	$
	$
	$
	$
	$
	$
	$
	$
	$
	$
	$

Name _____

Name _____

Our Picnic Blanket

Shopping for Clothes

 Understanding the Student Perspective

Many children see family members shopping for clothes, and children may be asked to try on clothes in the store to make sure they fit. As with buying groceries, students are just starting to develop a sense of value and worth. Unlike food, which is gone after one use, clothing is generally expected to last longer and be worn many times. How long depends on how fast the child grows and how fast the clothes wear out. Whether clothes shopping is done in person or online, at a clothing store, a thrift store, or a yard sale, it involves making choices about features such as fit, color, warmth, durability, and cost.

This unit helps students distinguish what is most important to them as they make choices about what to buy. The math skills used in this unit include skip counting, addition, subtraction, and currency.

 Pacing/Lesson Plan

1. Distribute a copy of Summer Shirts on pages 44 and 45 to each student. Read the story aloud to the class as students follow along. Note that the bold words in the story are defined on page 46.

2. Use the Discussion Questions on page 43 to lead a discussion with the class after reading Summer Shirts.

3. Distribute a copy of the Words to Know on page 46 to each student. Introduce the vocabulary words, rephrasing or explaining as needed. Then read the directions for the vocabulary practice and have students complete the activity.

4. Distribute a copy of Dressing for the Weather on page 47 to each student. Read each item to students and provide support as they complete the activity.

5. Distribute a copy of Dina's Shopping Trip on page 48 to each student. Make play-money bills or other counters available for students. Read each item to students and provide support as they complete the activity.

6. Distribute a copy of Omar's New Clothes on page 49 to each student. Make play-money bills or other counters available for students. Read each item to students and provide support as they complete the activity.

7. Have students do the Trip to the Clothing Store activity on page 50. To prepare, make copies of Clothing and Prices on page 51, I Can Show My Work on page 52, and What Should I Wear? on page 53. Gather the other needed materials.

Discussion Questions

Use these questions to lead a discussion with the class after reading the story. You may also wish to add your own questions.

- Have you ever gone shopping for clothes? Tell what happened. Why did you need new clothes?

- What kinds of clothes do you need for summer? What kinds of clothes do you need for winter?

- **Features** are parts of something. What features would you look for when you buy a coat? What features would you look for when you buy a pair of shoes?

- Do you think the price of something is an important feature? Why or why not?

 Materials

For word problems on pages 48 and 49:
- play-money bills (see pages 10 and 11)
- counters (optional)

For Trip to the Clothing Store on pages 50–53—each student needs:
- Clothing and Prices, page 51
- I Can Show My Work, page 52
- What Should I Wear? page 53
- play money bills (see pages 10 and 11)
- scissors
- crayons, colored pencils, or markers
- glue or tape

 Vocabulary Words

discount	expensive	feature
price tag	sale	

Summer Shirts

Asha looked out her window. Another sunny day! Summer was almost here! Asha looked in her closet. All her tops were sweaters or long-sleeved shirts. At breakfast, Asha asked her mom if they could go shopping for a shirt with short sleeves.

"Okay," said Mom. "But before we go, let's think about what we're looking for. I know you want a shirt with short sleeves. What others **features** do you want your new shirt to have?"

Asha thought for a minute. "It should be light, not heavy. I don't want it to make me hot."

"Great," said Mom. "Anything else?"

Asha thought some more. "It needs to be the right size," she said. "Some of my winter shirts are getting a little tight!"

"Well, you are growing," Mom said. "Let's make sure that the shirt is not too **expensive**. We can spend $20 on this shirt."

My summer shirt:
has short sleeves
feels light
fits just right
$20 or less

They made a list of all the features they would look for.

Then they drove to a clothing store. A big sign out front said "**Discount** Day"!

"Look at that!" said Mom. "They're having a **sale**! That means some of the items will have a lower price today!"

Financial Literacy Lessons and Activities • EMC 3122 • © Evan-Moor Corporation

Shopping for Clothes

Asha walked around the store. She found a shirt with a cool design. "How about this?" she asked her mom.

Mom pointed to their list. "Do the features match?" she asked.

"Oh," said Asha. "I guess not. It has long sleeves. But I like the pictures on it!" Asha put it back. Then she found some shirts with short sleeves. They came in lots of different colors.

"How about these?" Asha asked.

"Hmmm," said Mom, looking at their list. "These shirts all have short sleeves and they feel light. That's great! Now what about the other features?"

"Let's see if they fit," said Asha. She went to the fitting room and tried on different sizes. The medium fit her well.

"Okay," said Mom. "There's one last thing to check." Mom looked at the **price tag** and showed it to Asha.

"It's $20!" said Asha. "Perfect!"

"Wait!" said Mom. "It has a red sticker on it. That means it has a discount today. Instead of being $20, today it is $10!"

"You mean," said Asha, "I can get two shirts?"

"Yes!" answered Mom.

"Thanks so much, Mom!" said Asha. "Summer weather, here I come!"

Name _____

Words to Know

feature	an important part of something
expensive	costing a lot of money
discount	a lower price
sale	a time when prices are lower
price tag	a label that shows how much something costs

Read the word. Then write it in the sentence. Read the sentence.

feature   The best _____ of this coat is that it is warm.

expensive   Those jeans are too _____!

discount   If we wait one more day, we can buy this bike at a _____.

sale   Let's go to today's big _____.

price tag   The _____ says this shirt costs only $6.

Name _____

Dressing for the Weather

Read the questions. Draw or write your answers.

1. Draw yourself in summer. Show what clothes you wear then.

2. Pretend that you are getting new boots for winter. Circle the feature that you care about most. Tell why.

low price   **look nice**   **feel warm**   **stay dry**   **fit well**

This feature is most important because _____

_____

_____.

Name _____

Dina's Shopping Trip

Dina is buying some clothes. Read each word problem.
Write or draw your answers.

1. Dina has $40. She wants to buy this hat,
top, and coat. Look at the price tags.

Can Dina buy them all? Circle.

yes　　**no**

Explain why or why not. _____

_____

2. Dina comes back to the store a week later
during a sale. The coat now costs $20. The
other prices haven't changed. Now how
much do the hat, top, and coat cost in all?

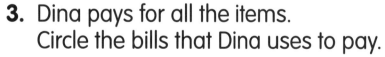

$ _____

3. Dina pays for all the items.
Circle the bills that Dina uses to pay.

Name _____

Omar's New Clothes

Omar is going shopping. Read each word problem. Write your answers.

1. Count Omar's money. How much does he have in all?

$ _____

---

2. At the clothing store, Omar finds some jeans. Usually they cost $35, but today they have a discount. They cost only $20. If Omar buys the jeans today, how much money will he save?

$ _____

---

3. Omar tells his friends about the sale. He and his friends Max and Jay each buy 1 pair of the $20 jeans. How much do the three friends spend in all?

$ _____

Trip to the Clothing Store

Tell the class that they will go shopping for clothes. They will have $80 to spend.

WHAT YOU NEED

- Clothing and Prices, page 51
- I Can Show My Work, page 52
- What Should I Wear? page 53
- play money ($80 per student)
- scissors
- glue or tape
- crayons, colored pencils, or markers

WHAT YOU DO

1. Distribute a copy of Clothing and Prices to each student. Tell students to color the clothing. Then have them cut out all the items and the price tags at the top of the page. Have them attach a price to the back of each item. Students can decide which price to put on which item.

2. Show students the area of the classroom that will be the Clothing Store. Have students place their cut-out clothing items in the Clothing Store.

3. Next, distribute play money and a copy of I Can Show My Work to each student.

4. Tell students to go to the Clothing Store and choose clothes they want to buy. They have $80. They do not have to spend all of it. They can keep track of their spending in two ways:

   - **play money:** they can count out the play money they are spending as they choose each item

   - **I Can Show My Work:** they can use the sheet as scratch paper, writing down the prices and adding to find their total

5. Distribute a copy of What Should I Wear? Have students attach the clothing they chose to the body shape. They can use crayons, colored pencils, or markers to add their face and hair and to decorate the background.

EXAMPLE

Show the class an example of a completed project.

Clothing and Prices

$15	$35	$40
$20	$20	$20

Name _____

I Can Show My Work

My total: $_____

Financial Literacy Lessons and Activities • EMC 3122 • © Evan-Moor Corporation

What Should I Wear?

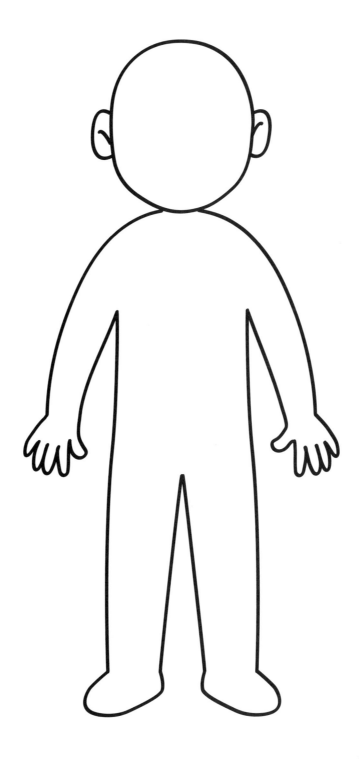

Earning Money in Your Family

 Understanding the Student Perspective

Children may not have a sense of how much things cost since parents likely provide everything for them from the time they are born. They may have even less sense of the effort needed to afford what parents buy. As children get older, they often want certain things. Earning money and then spending it helps them understand its value. If they know how hard they worked to earn money, they may put more thought into how they use it and may better appreciate gifts.

Children often have opportunities to receive money from family members. Money given as a gift or earned from chores helps develop skills in saving and making spending decisions.

This unit helps students understand that money has value and make connections between working and buying something they want. The math skills used in this unit include skip counting, addition, subtraction, and using currency.

 Pacing/Lesson Plan

1. Distribute a copy of A Race to the Finish on pages 56 and 57 to each student. Read the story aloud to the class as students follow along. Note that the bold words in the story are defined on page 58.

2. Use the Discussion Questions on page 55 to lead a discussion with the class after reading A Race to the Finish.

3. Distribute a copy of the Words to Know on page 58 to each student. Introduce the vocabulary words, rephrasing or explaining as needed. Then read the directions for the vocabulary practice and have students complete the activity.

4. Distribute a copy of Chore Time on page 59 to each student. Read each item to students and provide support as they complete the activity.

5. Distribute a copy of Saving to Buy on page 60 to each student. Make play-money bills or other counters available for students. Read each item to students and provide support as they complete the activity.

6. Distribute a copy of Gleb's Allowance on page 61 to each student. Make play-money bills or other counters available for students. Read each item to students and provide support as they complete the activity.

7. Have students play Spin to Earn on page 62. To prepare, make copies of the Game Board on page 63, the Spinner on page 64, and the Chance Cards on page 65 for each group. Cut out the Chance Cards. Gather the other needed materials.

Discussion Questions

Use these questions to lead a discussion with the class after reading the story. You may also wish to add your own questions.

- What did Gianni's sister say he could do to earn money? *[ask Mom for chores]*

- Do you have chores at home? If you do, what is your favorite chore? What is your least favorite chore?

- Do you get an allowance? If so, what do you spend it on?

- In the story, Gianni could earn $1 for sweeping the floor. He could earn $3 for weeding the garden or walking the dog. Why do you think Gianni's mom paid more for some chores than others?

- Do you think it is easy or hard to save money? Why or why not?

 Materials

For word problems on pages 60 and 61:
- play-money bills (see pages 10 and 11)
- counters (optional)

For Spin to Earn on pages 62–65—each group of 4 or 5 students needs:
- Game Board, page 63
- Spinner, page 64
- Chance Cards, page 65
- at least $40 in play money (see page 10)
- a paper clip
- a pencil
- 4 or 5 game pieces (small items such as Snap Cubes or counters) in different colors

 Vocabulary Words

afford	allowance	chore
earn	save	

A Race to the Finish

Gianni saw a remote-control car at the store. He imagined himself racing it around the neighborhood. He asked his mom if she would get it for him. She shook her head. "If you want it, you'll have to buy it on your own."

"But Mom, it's $40!" said Gianni. He was upset. He didn't think that he'd ever have that much money. He didn't get his allowance until the end of the month. And his **allowance** was only $10. How would he ever be able to **afford** the car?

When Gianni got back home, his sister Mariella asked him, "What's bothering you?" He told her about the car.

"You're going to get $10 at the end of the month," she reminded him. "So you really only need $30 more."

"That's still a lot of money," said Gianni, frowning.

"Ask Mom for some **chores**," said Mariella. "Then you can **earn** the money you need. That's how I get the money to buy those mystery books I love, remember?"

The next day, Gianni asked his mom for some chores. She wrote down what chores he could do and how much he would earn for each chore.

"Thanks!" said Gianni. Then he looked at the chart more closely. "Oh no!" he said. "Even if I do everything on this list, I still won't be able to earn $30!"

Gianni's Jobs

Sweep the floor	$1
Water the plants	$2
Clean the sinks	$2
Weed the garden	$3
Walk the dog	$3

Mariella looked up from her book. "Then you'll have to earn a little at a time and **save** your money until you have enough."

Gianni sighed. Then he thought to himself, "Ready, set, go!" He got to work. He worked hard! He made $5 that day. The next weekend he made $9.

By the end of the month, Gianni had already saved $35! With his allowance of $10, he had $45 total to spend. At the store, he bought the remote-control car and something extra, too.

When he got home, he gave his sister the next book in her mystery series. Her eyes opened wide. "Gianni, you're the best!"

Gianni smiled. It felt good to earn his own money. It felt even better spending it on things he wanted.

Name _____

Words to Know

allowance	money that parents give to children
afford	to be able to buy something
chore	a small job done at home
earn	to get money for doing a job
save	to keep money instead of spending it

Read the word. Then write it in the sentence. Read the sentence.

allowance   I get an _____ every week.

afford   I can't _____ to buy that right now.

chore   Sweeping is my favorite _____.

earn   I'll _____ $20 if I do all these chores!

save   I will _____ up to buy something big.

Name _____

Chore Time

Read the items. Draw or write your answers.

1. Pretend that you need to do 2 chores. Check the boxes next to the 2 chores you would choose.

☐ water the garden   ☐ sweep the floor

☐ brush the cat   ☐ clean your room

☐ fold the clean towels   ☐ feed the goldfish

2. Your room is messy. You need to clean it. Draw how your room looks before you clean it. Now draw how your room looks after you clean it.

Before	After

Saving to Buy

Shalifa likes doing chores to earn money. Look at the list of chores.
Read each word problem. Write or draw your answers.

1. Shalifa did 2 chores today. She earned $7. Which chores did she do?

_____

_____

Shalifa's Chores	
Feed the dog	$1
Dust the shelves	$2
Dry the dishes	$3
Weed the garden	$5

2. Last week, Shalifa dried the dishes three times, fed the dog twice, and weeded the garden once. Draw how much money she made.

3. Shalifa wants to buy this jacket. She has saved $21 so far. What chores could she do to buy the jacket?

$30

Name _____

Gleb's Allowance

Gleb gets an allowance. Read each word problem. Write or draw your answers.

1. Gleb gets an allowance of $5 a week. Skip count to find out how much money he makes in 5 weeks.

$ _____

---

2. If Gleb does extra chores, his parents will give him $10 a week. Gleb does extra chores for 4 weeks. Check the box that shows how much money he makes after 4 weeks.

☐

☐

☐

☐

Spin to Earn

Tell the class that they will be playing a game called Spin to Earn in small groups.

SET-UP

- Put students into groups of 4 or 5.

- Gather materials: Each group needs a Game Board on page 63, a Spinner on page 64, a set of Chance Cards on page 65, play money in $1s totaling at least $40, a paper clip, a pencil, and a different game piece (a small item such as a Snap Cube or a counter) for each player.

- Show students how to use the spinner: Push a pencil into the center point of the spinner and through the end of the paper clip. Flick the paper clip and watch it spin.

- Tell students to put all the play money in a pile, called The Bank. Have students put the Chance Cards facedown in another pile.

- Have each player choose a game piece. Put all game pieces on the Game Board at START.

PLAY

The object of the game is to get to the end of the game with the most money.

On each turn, one player spins the spinner and moves his or her game piece the number of spaces shown on the spinner. If the player lands on a Chance space, he or she takes a Chance Card.

- If the card says **Allowance**, the player takes the amount shown on the card from The Bank.

- If the card says **Do a Chore**, the player acts out the chore shown. The other players try to guess the chore. If a player guesses correctly, the "actor" takes the amount shown on the card from The Bank. If no one guesses correctly after 3 tries, the "actor" tells the other players what the chore was but does not earn any money.

The game ends when a player reaches the FINISH space or when all Chance Cards have been played. All players count up their money. The player with the most money wins.

EXAMPLE

If needed, the teacher can demonstrate how to act out a chore.

- The teacher draws a card and acts out what is on the card as students try to guess the chore.

- If a student guesses correctly, the teacher takes the amount shown on the card from The Bank.

- If no one guesses correctly, the teacher repeats the action and explains how it shows the chore.

Earning Money in Your Family

Game Board

START

CHANCE

CHANCE

CHANCE

CHANCE

CHANCE

CHANCE

CHANCE

CHANCE

CHANCE

CHANCE

CHANCE

CHANCE

CHANCE

CHANCE

FINISH

Spinner

Put the end of a paper clip over the dot in the center of the spinner.
Put the point of a pencil through the paper clip. Now spin!

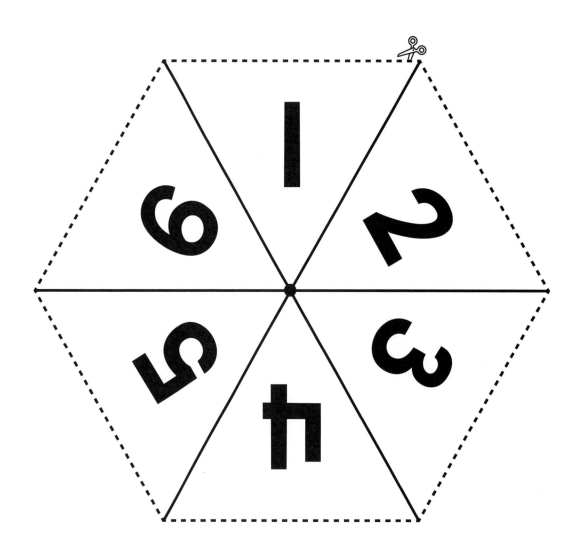

Chance Cards

Do a Chore	Do a Chore	Do a Chore	**Allowance**
sweep **$2**	walk the dog **$1**	pick apples **$3**	**$1**
Do a Chore make the bed **$1**	**Do a Chore** dust tables **$2**	**Do a Chore** set the table **$1**	**Do a Chore** fold towels **$2**
Do a Chore clean the mirror **$2**	**Allowance** **$1**	**Do a Chore** take out the trash **$3**	**Do a Chore** pick up toys **$1**
Do a Chore vacuum **$4**	**Do a Chore** wash the dog **$3**	**Do a Chore** water the plants **$1**	**Do a Chore** rake the leaves **$3**

Saving Money

 Understanding the Student Perspective

Children may have some experience with both using money and saving money at a young age. They might sip part of a drink now and save the rest to drink later. They might save new shoes for a special occasion. They might spend some money now and save some to use later. However, if children want to buy something that costs more than they have, they may not realize that they can continue adding to their money until they have enough to buy it. Saving small amounts of money lets them buy a larger item. Setting a goal and making a plan to reach the goal can help people save enough to buy things that they can't afford right now.

This unit helps students understand that saving comes from money you receive that you don't spend. People save to buy something in the future. Money can be saved in a bank or at home in a special place. The math skills used in this unit include skip counting, addition, subtraction, and using currency.

 Pacing/Lesson Plan

1. Distribute a copy of Saving for the Future on pages 68 and 69 to each student. Read the story aloud to the class as students follow along. Note that the bold words in the story are defined on page 70.

2. Use the Discussion Questions on page 67 to lead a discussion with the class after reading Saving for the Future.

3. Distribute a copy of the Words to Know on page 70 to each student. Introduce the vocabulary words, rephrasing or explaining as needed. Then read the directions for the vocabulary practice and have students complete the activity.

4. Distribute a copy of Something Special on page 71 to each student. Read each item to students and provide support as they complete the activity.

5. Distribute a copy of Alma's Guitar on page 72 to each student. Make play-money bills or other counters available for students. Read each item to students and provide support as they complete the activity.

6. Distribute a copy of Darryl's Allowance on page 73 to each student. Make play-money coins and bills or other counters available for students. Read each item to students and provide support as they complete the activity.

7. Have students play Robot for Sale! on page 74. To prepare, make copies of the Spinner on page 75, the Save or Spend Cards on page 76, and Beep! Bop! Boop! on page 77. Cut out the cards. Gather the other needed materials.

Financial Literacy Lessons and Activities • EMC 3122 • © Evan-Moor Corporation

Discussion Questions

Use these questions to lead a discussion with the class after reading the story. You may also wish to add your own questions.

- What did Oksana almost spend her money on? *[a bouncy ball]*
  Why do you think she changed her mind?

- When you get money, do you usually save it or spend it right away?

- Have you ever saved up to buy something? If so, tell about it.

- In the story, Oksana and Oleg save up to buy a magnifying glass. If you could save up for something special, what would it be?

- Do you think it is hard or easy to save money? Why or why not?

 Materials

For word problems on pages 72 and 73:

- play-money coins and bills (see pages 10 and 11)
- counters (optional)

For Robot for Sale! on pages 74–77—each group of students needs:

- Spinner, page 75
- Save or Spend Cards, page 76
- $60 in play money (see page 10)
- a paper clip
- a pencil
- Beep! Bop! Boop!, page 77, to display for the class

 Vocabulary Words

future	goal	savings
spend	total	

Name _____

Saving for the Future

Oksana and Oleg are twins. On their birthday, they each got a card from their grandparents with $8 inside.

Their dad offered to take them to the toy store. Oksana loves science. She wanted a big magnifying glass. She saw one at the store. But the price was $30.

Oleg also loves science. He noticed the magnifying glass and walked over to Oksana. "Wow, that's so cool," he said. "I want one, too!"

"It costs too much," said Oksana sadly.

"We can put our money together!" said Oleg.

"But $8 plus $8 is still only $16," said Oksana. "It's not enough. I'll just buy something small instead." She picked up a bouncy ball. "Like this. I'll just get this."

"No! You won't play with that," said Oleg. "Let's save our money for what we really want."

"What do you mean?" asked Oksana.

"Let's not **spend** our money right away," said Oleg. "Let's keep it in a can for the **future**. Then when we get more money, we can add it to the can until we have enough for the magnifying glass."

"It's a deal!" said Oksana. They shook hands. Then they told their dad they were ready to go home.

At home, they did some chores. They did chores the next weekend, too. Whenever they earned money, they added it to their **savings**.

One day, they took the money out of the can and counted it. The **total** was $50 dollars! They had reached their **goal**! The next day, they went to the toy store and bought the magnifying glass.

As soon as they got home, the twins went outside. Oleg picked a bunch of leaves, all different kinds. Oksana caught some insects in a jar. They looked at everything through the magnifying glass. It looked amazing!

"I'm proud of us," said Oksana.

"Me, too," said Oleg. "What should we save up for next?"

"Maybe a car?" joked their dad.

"How about a microscope?" said Oksana.

Oksana and Oleg shook hands.

"It's a deal!" they said.

Name _____

Words to Know

spend	to pay money to buy something
future	a time that hasn't happened yet
savings	money that someone has saved
total	the amount of everything added together
goal	something you want to do or have

Read the word. Then write it in the sentence. Read the sentence.

spend   Don't _____ all your money
on candy.

future   I'll be an astronaut in the _____ .

savings   Joy added $1 to her _____
every week.

total   Nico paid a _____ of $50 for his
new clothes.

goal   My _____ is to run to the park
and back home.

Name _____

Something Special

Read the items. Draw or write your answers.

1. If you could save money to buy something special, what would you buy? Draw a picture.

2. Pretend that you are at a toy store. You have $2. You can buy stickers or a pen today. Or you could save to buy a drum or an art set for $40 in the future. Circle the item you would choose.

I chose it because _____.

Name _____

Alma's Guitar

Alma wants to save money to buy a guitar.
Read each word problem. Write your answers.

1. Alma wants to buy this guitar. It costs $50.
She has $14. How much more does she
need to save?

$_____

2. Alma walks dogs to make money. She gets
$5 for every dog she walks. She walks 8 dogs.
How much money does she make?

$_____

3. Does Alma have enough money for the guitar now? Circle.

yes　　**no**

Explain. _____

_____

Name _____

Darryl's Allowance

Sometimes Darryl saves his allowance. Other times he spends it.
Read each word problem. Write or draw your answers.

1. Darryl gets an allowance. He gets $10 each week.
If he saves his allowance for 3 weeks, how much
will he save?

$_____

2. Darryl wants to buy a baseball cap,
a soccer ball, and a T-shirt. How much
money does he need to save?

$_____

3. Darryl decides to buy only a small toy car today. The car costs 75¢.
Check the box that shows the amount Darryl pays at the store.

Saving Money

Robot for Sale!

Tell the class that they will be playing a game to save money to buy a robot.

SET-UP

- Put students in groups of 4.

- Gather materials: Each group needs $60 of play money in $1s, a paper clip, a pencil, the Spinner on page 75, and a set of Save or Spend Cards on page 76. Also have one copy of Beep! Bop! Boop! on page 77 to display on a wall of the room.

- Show students how to use the spinner: Push a pencil into the center point of the spinner and through the end of the paper clip. Flick the paper clip and watch it spin.

- Tell students to put all the play money in a pile, called The Bank. Have students put the Save or Spend Cards facedown in another pile.

- Call students' attention to the Beep! Bop! Boop! sign in the room.

PLAY

The object of the game is to save enough money to buy the robot shown on the sign in the room. The player who saves $15 first buys the robot and wins the game.

On each turn, one player draws a Save or Spend Card and reads it.

- If it says **You Save**, the player spins the spinner to see how much he or she gets. The player takes that amount from The Bank.

- If it says **You Spend**, the player spins the spinner to see how much he or she spends. The player puts that amount back in The Bank. If the player doesn't have enough, he or she puts in everything.

If players run out of Save or Spend Cards, they collect all the cards from the players, mix them up, and place them facedown in a new pile.

Players count their money as they play. When a player thinks he or she can buy the robot, the player says "Try to buy!" at the beginning of his or her next turn. The player counts his or her money while the other players watch. If it's enough, the player says "Beep! Bop! Boop!" and wins the robot!

Saving Money

Spinner

Put the end of a paper clip over the dot in the center of the spinner.
Put the point of a pencil through the paper clip. Now spin!

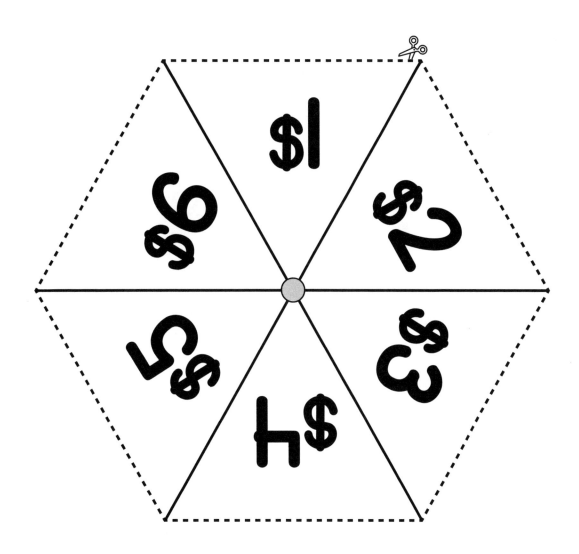

Save or Spend Cards

You walked the dog.	You dried the dishes.	You bought a book.	You sold lemonade.
You Save	You Save	You Spend	You Save
You swept the floor.	You bought candy.	You raked the leaves.	You got a money gift.
You Save	You Spend	You Save	You Save
You sold cookies.	You took out the trash.	You bought a ball.	You cleaned your room.
You Save	You Save	You Spend	You Save
You got your allowance.	You bought a game.	You folded laundry.	You sold your old toys.
You Save	You Spend	You Save	You Save

Financial Literacy Lessons and Activities • EMC 3122 • © Evan-Moor Corporation

Beep! Bop! Boop!

$15

Paying at a Restaurant

Understanding the Student Perspective

Children may have noticed that when a meal is served at home, their choices may be limited. One or both parents are busy preparing the meal and then cleaning up afterward. At a restaurant, there are more food choices, and children have more time with their parents. While children may notice that parents pay to eat out, they may not notice how it is different from paying in a store. They also might realize that the cost of a restaurant meal is usually more than a home-cooked meal since diners are also paying for the services involved (cooking, serving, cleaning).

This unit helps students understand some differences between eating at home and eating at a restaurant. The math skills used in this unit include skip counting, addition, subtraction, and using currency.

Pacing/Lesson Plan

1. Distribute a copy of A Delicious Surprise on pages 80 and 81 to each student. Read the story aloud to the class as students follow along. Note that the bold words in the story are defined on page 82.

2. Use the Discussion Questions on page 79 to lead a discussion with the class after reading A Delicious Surprise.

3. Distribute a copy of the Words to Know on page 82 to each student. Introduce the vocabulary words, rephrasing or explaining as needed. Then read the directions for the vocabulary practice and have students complete the activity.

4. Distribute a copy of My Menu on page 83 to each student. Read each item to students and provide support as they complete the activity.

5. Distribute a copy of Breakfast at Sam's Café on page 84 to each student. Make play-money coins and bills or other counters available for students. Read each item to students and provide support as they complete the activity.

6. Distribute a copy of Pizza Time on page 85 to each student. Make play-money bills or other counters available for students. Read each item to students and provide support as they complete the activity.

7. Have students do the Restaurant Role-Play activity on page 86. To prepare, make copies of the Roles on page 87, the Menu on page 88, and the Order Form and Check on page 89. Gather the other needed materials.

Discussion Questions

Use these questions to lead a discussion with the class after reading the story. You may also wish to add your own questions.

- Have you ever been to a restaurant? Tell about it.

- In the story, Ivan was unsure about trying something new. Have you ever tried a new food at a restaurant? What was it like?

- In this story, you read about the host and the server who work at a restaurant. What do they do? *[The host seats people. The server takes their order, brings their food, and takes their money. What other workers work at a restaurant? [cooks, dishwashers, cleaners]*

- Restaurant food usually costs more than food from a grocery store. Why do you think that is? *[You are paying for the work all the workers are doing in addition to the food.]*

 Materials

For word problems on pages 84 and 85:
- play-money coins and bills (see pages 10 and 11)
- counters (optional)

For Restaurant Role-Play on pages 86–89—each pair of students needs:
- Roles, page 87
- 2 copies of Menu, page 88
- 2 copies of Order Form and Check, page 89
- $15 in play money (see page 10)
- 2 paper plates
- pencils
- scissors
- tape

 Vocabulary Words

dish	host	menu
order	server	tip

A Delicious Surprise

Restaurant
*Captain
Camilla*
MENU

Ivan was excited. Today his family was going to a restaurant! "Can we get pizza?" he said.

"Since it's Mom's birthday, she gets to choose," said Dad.

"Let's go to that new restaurant called Captain Camilla!" said Mom. Ivan's older sister, Alona, seemed happy. But Ivan wasn't sure. What if he didn't like the food there?

"Don't worry," said Alona. "There will be lots of choices."

When they got there, the **host** greeted them. He led them to a table. After they sat down, he handed them each a **menu**. Ivan opened it up. There were a lot of choices! He had never heard of some of them. How would he decide?

"Read here," said Alona. She pointed to part of the menu. "It tells more about each **dish**." Ivan tried to read what it said, but he didn't know all the words. Mom asked what everyone wanted.

Alona said, "I want the seafood polenta."

"Great!" said Dad. "Let's get a family size and share it!"

"I don't know what that dish is," said Ivan.

Mom explained, "It's made from corn. It has all kinds of seafood on top. It's really good, but you can have something else."

Ivan pictured corn on the cob with a shrimp on top. "I'll just get fish and chips," he said.

Paying at a Restaurant

Name _____

A **server** came and asked what they wanted to **order**. Mom said, "We would like the family-sized seafood polenta and the fish and chips for my son." As the server went to tell the cook, Dad stood up and whispered something to her.

"What are you up to?" asked Mom. But Dad wouldn't answer.

A while later, the server brought the food. Ivan started to eat his crispy fish. But the polenta smelled so good! He asked to try it. Then he asked for more. "I'm glad we came here," he said.

Mom smiled. "It can be fun to try something new," she said. Just then, the server brought another dish. It was a dessert with a candle in it.

"Happy birthday!" said Dad.

"Was this what you were whispering about?" asked Mom. Dad nodded. Mom blew out the candle. "What a delicious surprise!" she said.

"It sure is a surprise," said Ivan. "It's not cake!"

Mom said, "You're right! It's called flan." She added, "and I bet you'll like it as much as the polenta!" Mom shared her flan with everyone. Then Dad paid the server for the meal. He also gave her a big **tip** to thank her for all her help.

Name

Words to Know

host	a person who seats people at a restaurant
menu	a list of choices
dish	a meal or food item
server	a person who helps people at a restaurant
order	to ask for something you want to eat
tip	money to give to a helpful person

Read the word. Then write it in the sentence. Read the sentence.

host   The _____ greeted us at the door.

menu   The _____ does not have many desserts.

dish   I chose a healthy _____.

server   The _____ asked what we wanted.

order   You can _____ now and pay later.

tip   I will make sure to leave a _____.

My Menu

Read the items. Draw or write your answers.

1. Pretend that you own a restaurant. Think of dishes you could serve at your restaurant. Draw them below.

2. Now make a menu. Write what dishes you will serve. Then write a price for each one.

Menu

Dish	Price
	$
	$
	$
	$
	$

Name _____

Breakfast at Sam's Café

Look at the menu. Read each word problem. Write your answers.

Breakfast	Drinks
pancakes $6	hot chocolate $3
ramen $4	tea $2
eggs $5	orange juice $3

1. Bae and her dad are going to have breakfast at Sam's Café.
Bae wants the ramen. Dad wants eggs and pancakes.
How much will their meal cost?

$ _____

2. Bae wants to use her own money to buy a hot chocolate.
Count the money she has.

Does she have enough?
Circle.

yes   **no**

Explain how you know.

_____

_____

      Financial Literacy Lessons and Activities • EMC 3122 • © Evan-Moor Corporation

Paying at a Restaurant   Name _____

Pizza Time

Sebastian and his family go to a restaurant. Read each word problem.
Write or draw your answers.

1. Sebastian and his family ordered 3 pizzas. Each pizza cost $10.
How much did they cost in all?

 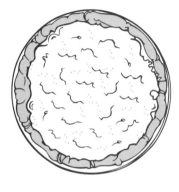 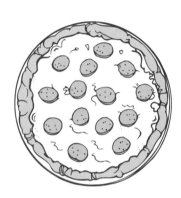

$ _____

2. Mom wanted to order salad, too. The total
cost of the 3 pizzas and the salad was $35.
How much did the salad cost?

$ _____

3. When they were done eating, Sebastian's mom left a tip
for the server. Look at the tip she left.

How much was the tip? $ _____

Restaurant Role-Play

Tell the class that they will work in pairs to do a role-play at a pretend restaurant. One student will be the customer, and one will be the server.

WHAT YOU NEED

- Roles, page 87, cut as indicated
- Menu, page 88
- Order Form and Check, page 89
- play money ($15 in $1s per student)
- pencils
- paper plates
- scissors
- tape

WHAT YOU DO

1. Put the students in pairs. One student is the customer, and the other is the server.

2. Give each **customer** the following: $15 in play money and a copy of the Customer Role.

   Give each **server** the following: a copy of the Menu, a copy of the Order Form and Check, a pencil, and a copy of the Server Role.

   Place the paper plates, scissors, and tape at a station for the servers to use after taking the customer's order.

3. Explain that students will pretend to be in a restaurant for lunch. Briefly explain each role and point out their Role sheets, which they can look at if they need help.

4. Role-play starts with servers giving a Menu to their customer and letting the customer read it. Then they ask what 3 things the customer would like to eat today. Customers point to what they want and tell the server. Have the server write the items and prices on the Order Form and Check and take the Menu.

5. The servers cut out each ordered item and tape them to a paper plate. Customers can read or do something else fun while they wait. Servers bring the plates to the customers. While the customers pretend to eat, the servers add up the prices and write the total on the Order Form and Check.

6. Servers give the customers their Order Form and Check. The customers use their play money to give the server the correct total shown on the check plus a tip.

7. Switch roles and repeat.

Paying at a Restaurant

Customer Role

Step 1	Step 2	Step 3	Step 4

Read the menu.	Tell the server what you want.	Eat the food.	Pay for the food and give a tip.

Server Role

Step 1	Step 2	Step 3	Step 4

Give the customer a menu.	Write the order and the prices.	Make and serve the food.	Give the customer the check.

Menu

sandwich $5	fries $2	coffee or tea $2
burrito $5	rice $2	juice $2
pizza slice $5	apple slices $1	milk $2
miso soup $3	beans $2	milkshake $5
ramen $3	salad $2	hot chocolate $3

Name _____

Order Form and Check

Food Item	Price
1. _____	$ _____
2. _____	$ _____
3. _____	$ _____
Total:	$ _____

Raising Money to Help Others

 Understanding the Student Perspective

Some children may not have experienced or seen hardship. They might assume that everyone in their community has their needs met with the same resources that they have. They may not realize that ongoing needs, such as food banks, animal shelters, and youth arts programs, are funded by contributions and volunteers. Other needs arise following an emergency, such as a house fire, medical treatment, or natural disaster. Communities often respond by fundraising to help out those in need.

Help can look different depending on the situation or emergency. Individuals and charities can provide resources for people who need help getting food or housing, have an illness or injury, or are recovering from a natural disaster.

This unit helps students understand how raising money can help provide food, water, shelter, and other necessities to those in need. The math skills used in this unit include skip counting, addition, subtraction, and using currency.

 Pacing/Lesson Plan

1. Distribute a copy of Rakhee to the Rescue on pages 92 and 93 to each student. Read the story aloud to the class as students follow along. Note that the bold words in the story are defined on page 94.

2. Use the Discussion Questions on page 91 to lead a discussion with the class after reading Rakhee to the Rescue.

3. Distribute a copy of the Words to Know on page 94 to each student. Introduce the vocabulary words, rephrasing or explaining as needed. Then read the directions for the vocabulary practice and have students complete the activity.

4. Distribute a copy of How Would You Help? on page 95 to each student. Read each item to students and provide support as they complete the activity.

5. Distribute a copy of Soraya's Bake Sale on page 96 to each student. Make play-money bills or other counters available for students. Read each item to students and provide support as they complete the activity.

6. Distribute a copy of Staying Warm in Winter on page 97 to each student. Make play-money bills or other counters available for students. Read each item to students and provide support as they complete the activity.

7. Have students do the Donate Today! activity on page 98. To prepare, make copies of the Cause Cards on page 99, Our Cause on page 100, and Create a Flier on page 101. Gather the other needed materials.

Discussion Questions

Use these questions to lead a discussion with the class after reading the story. You may also wish to add your own questions.

- What problem were Rakhee and her classmates worried about? *[hunger]*
  If you could help with a problem in your community, what would it be?

- Have you or your family ever donated to a food bank or volunteered at a food bank? Tell about it.

- The students in the story raised money with a talent show fundraiser. If you were going to raise money to help people, how would you do it?

- Have you ever helped out with a cause? Did you help by giving money or in some other way? Tell about the cause and how you helped.
  (If needed, give examples of causes, such as poverty; homelessness; cure for cancer; caring for the environment; victims of flooding, fire, hurricane, tornado, or earthquake; stray animals; any causes that affect your region.)

 Materials

For word problems on pages 96 and 97:
- play-money bills (see pages 10 and 11)
- counters (optional)

For Donate Today! on pages 98–101—each pair of students needs:
- Cause Cards, page 99
- Our Cause, page 100
- Create a Flier, page 101
- pencils
- tape or glue
- crayons, markers, or colored pencils
- $15 in play money (see pages 10 and 11)
- a shoebox, a tray, or an envelope to serve as a donation box

 Vocabulary Words

cause	charge	donate
flier	food bank	fundraiser

Rakhee to the Rescue

On the way to school, Rakhee and her dad were listening to the radio. The news came on. A reporter was talking about hunger. "Sadly, some people here in Cove Meadow do not have enough to eat. Some people are too old or too sick to work. Some can't find a job. And some are children." He said that people who wanted to help could **donate** food or money to the **food bank**.

"I thought banks just had money," said Rakhee. "Do they keep food in there, too?"

Dad smiled and said, "A food bank is a place that collects food. Then it gives the food to people who need it."

"Then why did the man on the radio say that people could give money?" Rakhee wondered.

Dad explained, "The food bank buys more food with the money. They can buy whatever they need more of."

At school, the class wrote in their journals. Rakhee wrote about the food bank. Her teacher, Ms. Benson, asked if anyone wanted to share. Rakhee raised her hand. She read what she wrote out loud.

The class started talking about the food bank. Seth said, "It's sad that some people don't have enough to eat."

Then Dion raised his hand. "Maybe we can collect money to help them!" he said.

"What do you think?" Rakhee asked Ms. Benson.

"I think it's a great idea. Feeding people who are hungry is a good **cause**," said Ms. Benson. "After lunch today, let's brainstorm ways to collect money."

But the kids were so excited, they started brainstorming during lunch! They decided they would put on a talent show at school. The talent show would be a **fundraiser**. They would sell tickets and **charge** $5 for each one. Then they would donate all the money to the food bank.

Ms. Benson liked their plan. The next week, the kids got to work. They decided who would be in the show and what each student would do. They practiced their acts. They made tickets. They also made **fliers** to tell their town about the show.

On the night of the talent show, lots of families came. Rakhee played the piano. Seth told jokes. Dion danced. Everyone had a great time. Rakhee loved playing in front of people. But the best part was the next day, when they donated all the money they raised to the food bank.

Words to Know

donate	to give money or things to help others
food bank	a place that collects food for people who need it
cause	a reason for helping
fundraiser	a way to collect money for something
charge	to ask people to pay a certain amount of money
flier	a sheet that tells about an event or an item

Read the word. Then write it in the sentence. Read the sentence.

donate   I will _____ some clothes.

food bank   Ali helps out at the _____.

cause   My favorite _____ is helping homeless people.

fundraiser   This _____ will help lost pets get new homes.

charge   They _____ $10 for each pony ride.

flier   This _____ tells about the game.

How Would You Help?

Read the items. Draw or write your answers.

1. Pretend that you are donating a box of items to a child who needs warm clothes. Draw what you would put in the box.

2. Pretend that you want to collect money for children who need shoes. How would you do it? Write an idea.

_____

_____

Name_____

Soraya's Bake Sale

Some people's homes were damaged in a flood. Soraya wants to raise money to help them. She decides to have a bake sale. Read each word problem. Write your answers.

BAKE SALE

Prices

cookies	$2
muffins	$1
cupcakes	$3

1. Soraya is selling cookies, muffins, and cupcakes. Look at the price list that she made. Her first customer wants to buy 3 cookies, 2 muffins, and 1 cupcake. How much does he need to pay?

$_____

2. At the end of the day, Soraya gathers up all the money she collected. Count it. How much did she make?

$_____

Staying Warm in Winter

Some people don't have warm clothes for winter. Asher's class wants to help. Read each word problem. Write or draw your answers.

1. Asher's class wants to buy 10 winter hats for people who need them. Each hat costs $5. How much money does Asher's class need to raise?

$_____

2. Asher's class ends up raising $56. After they buy 10 hats, how much money will they have left over?

$_____

3. The class wants to use the extra money to buy scarves for people who need them. A scarf costs $2. How many scarves can Asher's class buy?

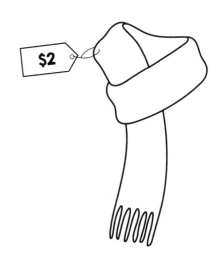

_____ scarves

Donate Today!

Tell the class that they will work in pairs to choose a cause and encourage others to donate to it.

WHAT YOU NEED

- Cause Cards, page 99
- Our Cause, page 100
- Create a Flier, page 101
- pencils
- tape or glue

- crayons, markers, or colored pencils
- play money ($15 per pair in $1s and $5s)
- a shoebox, a tray, or an envelope to serve as a donation box

WHAT YOU DO

1. Put students into pairs. Distribute one copy of Cause Cards; one copy of Our Cause; one copy of Create a Flier; and one donation box (shoebox, tray, or envelope) to each pair.

2. Have students read the Cause Cards or read the cards to students. Tell them they will choose a cause that is important to them. Have students talk with their partner to decide on a Cause Card. After they have decided, they cut out the card and attach it to the Our Cause sheet. Then they work together to answer the questions on the Our Cause sheet.

3. Have each pair make a sign on the Create a Flier sheet. The flier needs to do 3 things:

   - Tell what the cause is
   - Tell and show why the cause is important
   - Get people excited about the cause so they will donate to it

4. When students are ready, give $15 in play money to each pair. Have them display their fliers, Our Cause sheets, and donation boxes at their desks. Then they walk around the room and look at other pairs' fliers and Our Cause sheets. Have students decide with their partners where to donate their money. Here are the rules for donating:

   - You and your partner need to donate all your money
   - You CAN donate to one or more causes
   - You CAN'T donate to your own cause

5. When students are done, have them return to their desks, count the money they raised in their donation box, and write the total on the Our Cause sheet.

Cause Cards

An animal shelter needs money to pay for dog and cat food.

It is snowing outside, and some people need winter clothes.

A family's home burned down in a fire.

A music program for children needs money for instruments.

Some people don't have enough food.

The wildlife park needs to build a big living space for a new bear.

People who pick up litter need to buy trash bags and gloves.

Children at a hospital have no toys to play with.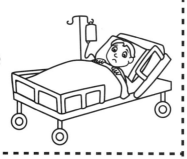

The art program for children needs money for art supplies.

The swings at the park are broken and need to be fixed.

Name _____

Name _____

Our Cause

Tape or glue your Cause Card here.

We collected $_____

Look at your Cause Card. Answer the questions.

1. Why is your cause important?

_____

_____

_____

_____

2. Why should people donate money to your cause?

_____

_____

_____

_____

Name _____

Name _____

Create a Flier

Create a flier so people will want to donate to your cause.

Paying to Go Places

Understanding the Student Perspective

Some students may have seen adults pay for bus or subway fare or purchase tickets at a movie theater. They may understand that travel and entertainment cost money. But there are many hidden costs involved in some travel and entertainment. A subscription to a monthly cable or streaming service costs money. Passes to ride public transportation cost money, as well, and even the family car requires money for fuel. Parking often has a separate cost.

This unit helps students understand that travel and entertainment cost money. The math skills used in this unit include skip counting, addition, and using currency.

Pacing/Lesson Plan

1. Distribute a copy of A Day with Dad on pages 104 and 105 to each student. Read the story aloud to the class as students follow along. Note that the bold words in the story are defined on page 106.

2. Use the Discussion Questions on page 103 to lead a discussion with the class after reading A Day with Dad.

3. Distribute a copy of the Words to Know on page 106 to each student. Introduce the vocabulary words, rephrasing or explaining as needed. Then read the directions for the vocabulary practice and have students complete the activity.

4. Distribute a copy of My Trip on page 107 to each student. Read each item to students and provide support as they complete the activity.

5. Distribute a copy of Mira Goes to the Beach on page 108 to each student. Make play-money bills or other counters available for students. Read each item to students and provide support as they complete the activity.

6. Distribute a copy of Let's Play Ball on page 109 to each student. Make play-money coins and bills or other counters available for students. Read each item to students and provide support as they complete the activity.

7. Have students do the Plan a Field Trip activity on page 110. To prepare, make copies of the Map on page 111, the Cost Cards on page 112, and the Trip Plan on page 113. Gather the other needed materials.

Discussion Questions

Use these questions to lead a discussion with the class after reading the story. You may also wish to add your own questions.

- Have you ever been to a museum, a movie or play, a concert, or a sporting event? Did someone pay for you to go to it? Do you remember getting a ticket or a stamp on your hand?

- In the story, the dad almost forgets his wallet. What might have happened if he had forgotten it? *[He wouldn't have been able to pay the bus fare or the museum fee. They'd have to get off the bus, go home, and get the wallet.]*

- What are some ways that people travel?

- Have you watched adults pay to travel? For example, have you seen adults buy gas at a gas station or pay for a plane ticket or a bus pass? Tell about it.

 Materials

For word problems on pages 108 and 109:
- play-money coins and bills (see pages 10 and 11)
- counters (optional)

For Plan a Field Trip on pages 110–113—each group of 3 or 4 students needs:
- Map, page 111
- Cost Cards, page 112
- Trip Plan, page 113
- play-money bills (see pages 10 and 11)
- scissors
- pencils
- blank paper
- colored pencils, crayons, or markers

 Vocabulary Words

entrance fee	fare	pass
passenger	travel	wallet

Name_____

A Day with Dad

Joaquina woke up and started to get ready for school. Then she remembered that there was no school today! It was a day off. Mom had to work at the hospital, but Dad would be home. They would get to spend the whole day together!

At breakfast, Dad asked Joaquina if she wanted to go to the Discovery Center. Joaquina almost jumped out of her chair. "Yes!" she said. The Discovery Center was a museum downtown. It had giant dinosaur models and some real dinosaur bones. Joaquina had always wanted to go there.

They were walking out the door when Dad stopped. "Whoops!" he said, "I forgot something!" He turned around and got his **wallet**.

"Do you really need that?" asked Joaquina. "We're not buying anything, are we?"

"We need money to **travel**. We need to pay the bus **fare** and the **entrance fee** at the museum."

"Oh," said Joaquina. "That *is* important!"

When they got on the bus, Dad put $6 in the machine at the front of the bus. It printed out two **passes**.

"These passes are good for the whole day," Dad told Joaquina. "We'll use them to ride home later."

Joaquina liked watching the other **passengers**. There were all kinds of people. An older man got on the bus with a big dog that took him to an empty seat. A lady got on with two babies. Some people listened to music. Some talked. Some looked at their phones.

When they got to the museum, Dad took his wallet out again. They went up to the front desk. The sign there said the entrance fee was $10 for adults and $5 for kids. Dad paid $15, and a woman stamped their hands.

"What's this stamp for?" Joaquina asked.

"It's so they know that we paid," said Dad.

Just then, Joaquina looked at the floor. It was painted with a trail of dinosaur footprints. "These are so cool!" she said. They followed the footprints to the main hall. It was full of huge dinosaur models. There was even a real Triceratops skeleton! Sounds of screeches, growls, and honks were playing. The walls were painted like a jungle. Joaquina couldn't believe it. "This place is the best!" she said.

"I'm just glad I remembered my wallet!" said Dad. They both laughed. Then they followed the footprints down the hall and into the land of the dinosaurs!

Land of the Dinosaurs

Name _____

Words to Know

wallet	a holder for money that folds
travel	to go to another place
fare	money that someone pays to ride
entrance fee	money paid to go into a place or an event
pass	a card or paper that lets you enter
passenger	someone who rides a bus, train, plane, or boat

Read the word. Then write it in the sentence. Read the sentence.

wallet I keep my money in my _____.

travel I will _____ to Italy.

fare The boat _____ is $12.

entrance fee Pay the _____ at the front desk.

pass This _____ lets you ride all day.

passenger The _____ sat down.

My Trip

Pretend that you can travel anywhere you want. Read the items.
Draw or write your answers.

1. If you could travel anywhere, where would you go?

I would go to _____.

2. How would you get there? Circle the way you would travel.

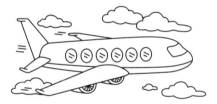  

3. Draw yourself there.

Name_____

Mira Goes to the Beach

Mira is going to the beach with her family. There are 2 adults, 1 child, and 1 baby in her family. Read each word problem. Write your answers.

1. Mira's family will ride the train to the beach. They need to buy tickets. Look at the train fares. How much will it cost for the whole family to ride the train?

$_____

Train Fares	
Adults	$40
Children	$20
Babies	Free

2. Mira's family will pay to stay in a cabin by the beach. It costs $64 each night. How much will it cost them to stay 2 nights?

$_____

Name _____

Let's Play Ball

Keenan is going to a baseball game with his mom. Read each word problem. Write or draw your answers.

1. Keenan and his mom drive to the game. They must pay to park. Look at the money Keenan's mom pays for parking. How much does she pay?

$ _____

---

2. Keenan and his mom need to buy tickets to get into the game. Tickets cost $35 each. Check the box that shows the money needed for 2 tickets.

☐

☐

☐

☐

Plan a Field Trip

Tell the class that they will plan a pretend field trip and figure out how much it costs.

WHAT YOU NEED

- Map, page 111
- Cost Cards, page 112
- Trip Plan, page 113
- play money ($100 per group)
- scissors
- pencils
- blank paper
- colored pencils, crayons, or markers

WHAT YOU DO

1. Divide students into groups of 3 or 4.

2. Distribute play money, pencils, and scissors to each group.

3. Have students look at the Map as you point to and describe each of the four field trip options (add fun details if you like). They can choose from these:

   - a soccer game at The Soccer Stadium

   - a music concert at The Concert Hall

   - a shark exhibit at The Aquarium

   - a cave tour at Candle Cave

   Let groups discuss the options and decide where their group will go.

4. Next, have students figure out how much their trip will cost. Give students the Map, the Cost Cards, and the Trip Plan page. Have them cut out the Cost Card for the trip they chose and use it to figure out their travel cost and their activity cost. Remind students that they need to figure out the cost for their whole group, not just for one person. Have them write the costs on the Trip Plan page.

5. Hand out blank paper to each student. Provide colored pencils, crayons, or markers. Have students draw themselves at their destination, enjoying their field trip.

Map

Cost Cards

The Concert Hall

Travel	Activity
bus fare: $5 for each person	tickets: $10 for each person

The Aquarium

Travel	Activity
parking fee: $20 for each group	entrance fee: $5 for each person PLUS tickets to shark feeding: $2 for each person

The Soccer Stadium

Travel	Activity
bus fare: $2 for each person	tickets: $20 for each person

Candle Cave

Travel	Activity
train fare: $10 for each person	entrance fee: $12 for each person

Paying to Go Places

Name _____   Name _____

Name _____   Name _____

Trip Plan

Read the questions. Write or draw your answers.

1. Where will your group go? _____

2. How much will your group's **travel** cost for everyone?

[ ]

3. How much will your group's **activity** cost for everyone?

[ ]

4. How much will your group's field trip cost **in all**?

[ ]

Using Banks

Understanding the Student Perspective

Children often save money that they receive as a gift or from their allowance. They may put their money in a pocket, a drawer, a jar, a basket, or a box in their bedroom. For small amounts of cash, a container at home works fine. They may not understand that adults and businesses handle much larger amounts of money, too much for a jar. Instead, they keep their money in banks, where it is safe.

Children may have seen a bank and wondered what it is for. They may have watched a parent withdraw money from an ATM or pay for goods using a card or check. They may think of a bank as a "money store," not realizing that their parents put in the money that comes out of the ATM. They may not know that the card used to pay for something accesses money in a parent's bank account. People have accounts at banks. There are many different kinds of accounts, such as savings and checking. People can deposit money into their accounts or withdraw money out of their accounts.

This unit helps students understand what a bank is and how people use banks to save money. The math skills used in this unit include comparing numbers, addition, subtraction, and using currency.

Pacing/Lesson Plan

1. Distribute a copy of Keeping Money Safe on pages 116 and 117 to each student. Read the story aloud to the class as students follow along. Note that the bold words in the story are defined on page 118.

2. Use the Discussion Questions on page 115 to lead a discussion with the class after reading Keeping Money Safe.

3. Distribute a copy of the Words to Know on page 118 to each student. Introduce the vocabulary words, rephrasing or explaining as needed. Then read the directions for the vocabulary practice and have students complete the activity.

4. Distribute a copy of Something Special on page 119 to each student. Read each item to students and provide support as they complete the activity.

5. Distribute a copy of Edgar's Account on page 120 to each student. Make play-money bills or other counters available for students. Read each item to students and provide support as they complete the activity.

6. Distribute a copy of Malia and Dad Go to the Bank on page 121 to each student. Make play-money bills or other counters available for students. Read each item to students and provide support as they complete the activity.

7. Have students do the Banking Role-Play activity on page 122. To prepare, make copies of the Role Cards on page 123, the Item Cards on page 124, and the Paycheck Labels on page 125. Cut them all out. Attach a Paycheck Label to each envelope and fill each envelope with the specified amount of money.

Discussion Questions

Use these questions to lead a discussion with the class after reading the story. You may also wish to add your own questions.

- What problem did Mallory have? *[Her money jar was full.]*

- If you had a lot of money, where would you keep it?

- Have you ever been to a bank? Tell about it.

- Why do you think many adults put their money in banks?

 Materials

For word problems on pages 120 and 121:
- play-money bills (see pages 10 and 11)
- counters (optional)

For Banking Role-Play on pages 122–125—each group of 3 students needs:
- Role Cards, page 123
- Item Cards, page 124
- Paycheck Labels, page 125
- 3 envelopes
- $80 of play money (see page 11)

 Vocabulary Words

account	bank	cash
deposit	teller	withdraw

Name _____

Keeping Money Safe

Mallory was saving her money to buy an art set. Whenever she earned money for chores, she put it in a jar. One day, the jar was full. Mallory asked Mom for a bigger jar. Mom looked around the house. "Hmmm," she said. "I'll have to get you one at the store."

Then Mallory thought of something. "Mom, where do you keep your money? You must have a really big jar for it!"

Mom laughed. "I don't keep my money in a jar, Mallory," Mom explained. "I keep my money in a **bank**."

"A bank?" asked Mallory.

"Yes," said Mom. "Banks keep money safe. Jars are good for small amounts of money. But when you are older, you will earn more money. You can keep that money safe by putting it in a bank."

Mallory looked confused. "Is a bank like a really, really, really big jar?"

Mom smiled. "I'll show you later today," she said.

That afternoon, they rode the bus to the bank. "This is where I keep my money," said Mom. "I have an **account** here. When I earn money at my job, I **deposit** it into my account."

They walked inside. A woman stood behind a counter. "That is a **teller**," Mom told Mallory. "When I earn money, I give it to a teller, and the teller puts it into my account."

"But what if you need some of it back?" asked Mallory. "What if you need to buy something?"

"Watch," said Mom. She told the teller she wanted to **withdraw** $20 from her account. The teller handed her $20 in **cash**.

"Oh! So that money came out of your account?" asked Mallory.

"Yes!" said Mom. "I can deposit money in a bank account. I can also withdraw money."

"I think I'm starting to understand this!" said Mallory.

"Now let's get you that jar!" said Mom. They stopped at a store and found a really big jar. Mom paid with the cash from the bank.

"Thanks, Mom," said Mallory. "This jar will be perfect— until I'm old enough for my own bank account!"

"Sounds good to me!" said Mom.

Name _____

Words to Know

bank	a place that keeps people's money safe
account	a record of how much money a person has
deposit	to put money in
teller	a person who helps customers at a bank
withdraw	to take money out
cash	money; coins and paper bills

Read the word. Then write it in the sentence. Read the sentence.

bank   She stopped at the _____ to get money.

account   You have $156 in your _____.

deposit   I'd like to _____ $20 today.

teller   The _____ handed me my money.

withdraw I need to _____ $50.

cash   I will pay for this shirt using _____.

Name _____

Something Special

Read the questions. Draw or write your answers.

1. Pretend that you are an adult. You have a job and a bank account. What special thing would you save money for? Draw it below.

2. Pretend that you have a bank account. You have $80 in your account. What will you do? Choose one.

☐ I will withdraw all my money to buy a bike now.

☐ I will keep my money in the bank to buy a computer later when I have enough money.

I chose it because _____

_____.

• EMC 3122 • Financial Literacy Lessons and Activities

Name _____

Edgar's Account

Edgar's parents have started a bank account for him. Read each word problem. Write or draw your answers.

1. Edgar has $40 in his account. He earns $10 for doing chores and deposits it into his account. Then he withdraws $20 to buy a board game. Next, he withdraws $12 to buy his mom a gift. How much money is left in his account?

$_____

2. Edgar decides to save up for something big. He starts putting $20 in his account every month. He does this for 3 months. How much does he deposit into his account?

$_____

Which of these items could Edgar buy now? Circle your answer.

Financial Literacy Lessons and Activities • EMC 3122 • © Evan-Moor Corporation

Name _____

Malia and Dad Go to the Bank

Malia goes to the bank with her dad. Read each word problem.
Write your answers.

1. Dad withdraws $40 from his account. He has $10 left in his account. How much money was in his account to start with?

$_____

---

2. The next time Malia goes to the bank with Dad, he makes a deposit. He hands this money to the teller.

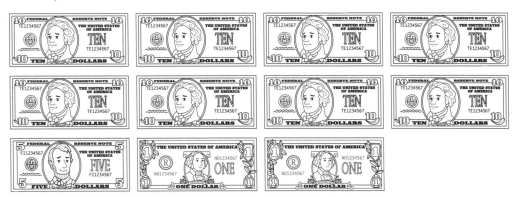

How much does he deposit? $_____

---

3. How much money is in Dad's account now? $_____

Banking Role-Play

Tell the class that they will do a banking role-play in small groups. One student will be the shopkeeper, one will be the teller, and one will be the customer.

WHAT YOU NEED

For each group of 3 students:

- Role Cards, page 123

- Item Cards, page 124

- Paycheck Labels, page 125, cut out and attached to the envelopes

- 3 envelopes containing play money in $10s in the following amounts: $40, $30, $10 (It doesn't matter which amount is in which "paycheck." The order should be random.)

WHAT YOU DO

1. Put students in groups of 3. Give each student a Role Card. One student is the Shopkeeper, one is the Teller, and one is the Customer. Give each Shopkeeper a set of Item Cards in a stack, facedown.

2. Give each Customer his or her first envelope (Paycheck 1). Explain that this is the money earned at his or her job this week. Have Customers count their money.

3. Have the Shopkeepers flip over the first Item Card and show it to their Customer and try to talk the Customer into buying the item. Explain the Customer's options:

   - The Customer **wants the item**. He or she pays the Shopkeeper and takes the Item Card. Then he or she deposits any extra money in the bank, handing it to the Teller.

   - The Customer **doesn't buy the item**. He or she deposits all the money in the bank, handing it to the Teller.

4. Give Customers Paychecks 2 and 3 and repeat as above.

Role Cards

Shopkeeper

- Shows an item to the customer and tries to sell it

Teller

- Takes money from the customer

Customer

- Buys items from the shopkeeper

- Deposits money with the teller

Item Cards

art set

$50

toy robot

$70

guitar

$60

bike

$80

stuffed animals

$20

ice cream sundae

$10

puzzle

$10

scooter

$40

Using Banks

Paycheck Labels

Paycheck 1

Paycheck 2

Paycheck 3

Paying at the Post Office

 Understanding the Student Perspective

The post office provides valuable services that let people communicate with others around the world. People use it to send gifts, receive goods bought online, handle bills and other important papers, and even communicate with friends and family. Much communication happens online these days, which students will likely be aware of. But long lines at post offices remind us that they are still important in our communities, and students may not know much about this resource.

The post office provides services for which a lot of effort is hidden from view. We pay for these services a little differently from items in a store, using stamps or paying postage by weight or speed of delivery. The sender pays, even though the recipient often receives the benefit.

This unit helps students understand how the postage we pay is used. It sheds light on the many unseen parts of a global service. The math skills used in this unit include addition, subtraction, and using currency.

 Pacing/Lesson Plan

1. Distribute a copy of A Stamp's Trip on pages 128 and 129 to each student. Read the story aloud to the class as students follow along. Note that the bold words in the story are defined on page 130.

2. Use the Discussion Questions on page 127 to lead a discussion with the class after reading A Stamp's Trip.

3. Distribute a copy of the Words to Know on page 130 to each student. Introduce the vocabulary words, rephrasing or explaining as needed. Then read the directions for the vocabulary practice and have students complete the activity.

4. Distribute a copy of Moving the Mail on page 131 to each student. Read each item to students and provide support as they complete the activity.

5. Distribute a copy of Carlos's Cards on page 132 to each student. Make play-money bills or other counters available for students. Read each item to students and provide support as they complete the activity.

6. Distribute a copy of Patty's Package on page 133 to each student. Make play-money coins and bills or other counters available for students. Read each item to students and provide support as they complete the activity.

7. Have students do the Post Office Role-Play activity on page 134. To prepare, make copies of the Postcards on page 135 (on cardstock if possible), the Stamps on page 136 (on label sheets if possible), and the Mail Drop Sign on page 137 and cut them out. Gather the other needed materials.

Discussion Questions

Use these questions to lead a discussion with the class after reading the story. You may also wish to add your own questions.

- Who is telling this story? *[a stamp]*

- Have you ever gone to the post office? If so, what did you do there?

- Who buys the stamp for a letter: the person who sends the letter or gets the letter? *[the sender]*
  What might happen if the person who gets the letter had to pay?
  [That person might not want to pay. Then the post office did the work but did not get paid for it.]

- In the story, name some of the kinds of workers who helped deliver the card to the man's mother.
  [the worker who sold the stamp, the workers who put mail in different boxes/put them on and off trucks and planes, drivers, the people who flew the plane, the worker who delivered the card]

- The worker at the post office weighed the card. She said it was extra big. If the card was smaller, do you think the stamp would cost more or less? Why?

 Materials

For word problems on pages 132 and 133:
- play-money coins and bills (see pages 10 and 11)
- counters (optional)

For Post Office Role-Play on pages 134–137—students need:
- play-money coins (see page 11)
- Postcards, page 135
- Stamps, page 136
- Mail Drop Sign, page 137
- a mail collection box or tray
- tape or glue if needed for attaching stamps

 Vocabulary Words

mail	package	shipping
stamp	weigh	

A Stamp's Trip

I am a **stamp**. People buy me to **mail** things far away. When someone sticks me onto a **package** or a letter, my adventure begins!

I see a man and a little boy in line at the post office. Maybe they will need me. "I need to buy a stamp," the man says. "I am sending this birthday card to my mom. She lives in Alaska."

That sounds exciting! I have never been to Alaska. I hope they pick me! "That card is extra big," says the post office clerk. She placed the card on a scale to **weigh** it. "**Shipping** this card costs 88 cents," she said. The man gave the clerk some coins. "Here you go," she said and gave me to the man!

The man handed the card and me to his son. "Peel the stamp off the paper. Then put it right here in the corner," he told his son. The son put my sticky side on the card. Then he dropped the card in the mailbox. I'm on my way!

Soon another worker took all the mail out of the box. He read the places we were going. He put us in different boxes. I am going to Alaska with a large square package and five letters. He put our box on a truck.

Paying at the Post Office

A worker drove the truck down many roads to the airport. It was noisy! Someone else put our box on a plane with many other boxes. Then the people who fly the plane came on board. We're going up to the sky!

We flew for many hours. I asked the other stamps in my box if they knew what they were mailing. The stamp on the package said, "I am helping a pretty glass bowl go to the person who bought it." One of the letter stamps said, "I'm sending good news to someone who won a prize." Another stamp said, "I'm bringing photos of a new baby to his great-grandparents."

Finally, the plane landed. A worker took our box and put each of us on a different mail truck. The driver drove through snow! He stopped at the address on my card and carried me to a little box by the door. A lady opened the card and smiled!

Name _____

Words to Know

stamp	a sticker that shows how much you paid
mail	to send something through the post office
package	an item sent to someone in a box
weigh	to find out how heavy something is
shipping	moving something to another place

Read the word. Then write it in the sentence. Read the sentence.

stamp   I will put a _____ on the letter.

mail   She will _____ your gift today.

package   There is a big _____ outside!

weigh   Let's _____ the book before we send it.

shipping   _____ this box costs less than $9.

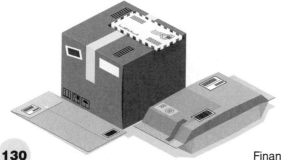

Name _____

Moving the Mail

Read the items. Draw or write your answers.

1. Draw the part of the stamp's trip that surprised you the most.

[ ]

2. Think of something that you or your family got in the mail.

What was it? _____

How would you get it without the mail?
- ☐ We would go pick up the item.
- ☐ A friend would bring it to us.
- ☐ We would have to make it.
- ☐ We wouldn't get it.

Name _____

Carlos's Cards

Carlos is sending cards to all his classmates. He goes to the post office to buy stamps. Read each word problem. Write or draw your answers.

1. Carlos took his cards to the post office. Each one needs a stamp. The total cost is $18. Look at the money Carlos has. Can he make exactly $18? Circle your answer.

yes   **no**

2. Carlos gives the post office clerk more than $18. Which bills should he give her? Circle them.

3. The post office clerk gives Carlos some money back in change. Draw or write how much she gives back.

Paying at the Post Office   Name _____

Patty's Package

Patty and her family went camping. Read each word problem.
Write or draw your answers.

1. Patty bought her friend a camping T-shirt. She took it to the
post office to mail it. The worker told Patty that she needs to
put the T-shirt in a box first. She buys a box with the coins below.

How much did the box cost? $ _____

2. The clerk weighed the
T-shirt and the box.
It costs $3 to send.
Draw dollar bills or
coins to show
what Patty pays.

3. Patty put the T-shirt in the box. She
wrote her friend's address on the box.
She gave the box to the worker. Count
all the money above. How much did
she pay in all at the post office?

$ _____

Post Office Role-Play

Tell the class that they will get to run a class post office or be a post office customer.

WHAT YOU NEED

- Postcards, page 135
- Stamps, page 136
- Mail Drop Sign, page 137
- a box, bin, or tray for mail collection
- tape or glue if needed to attach stamps
- play-money coins (40¢ to $1 per customer)
- play-money collection container
- pencils

WHAT YOU DO

1. Designate an area of the room for Post Office Clerks. Put the stamps and tape or glue there. Also have a container to collect the play money.

2. Put the Mail Drop Sign on the mail collection container and place it in another part of the room.

3. Assign each student's role: Customer, Post Office Clerk, or Letter Carrier.

4. Give each **Customer** a postcard, play money, and a pencil. Have them decide which classmate to send a postcard to and write that classmate's name on the right side of the postcard. Write a short note to that classmate on the left side of the postcard.

5. While the Customers are busy, show the post office workers their jobs:

   - **Post Office Clerks** sell stamps and collect money. They will also give out tape or glue, if needed.

   - **Letter Carriers** collect mailed cards from the Mail Drop and deliver them to the correct student.

6. As Customers finish their cards, they go to the post office to buy a stamp for 40¢. They put the stamp on their postcard and put the card in the Mail Drop. Letter Carriers collect the postcards and deliver them to the students.

Postcards

To:

_____

_____

_____

To:

_____

_____

_____

Stamps

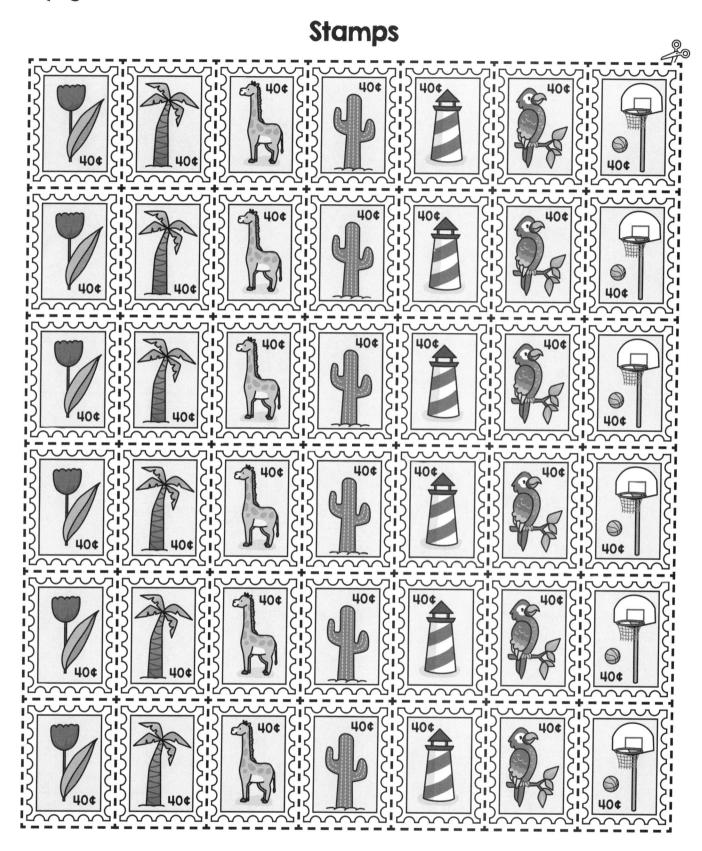

Financial Literacy Lessons and Activities • EMC 3122 • © Evan-Moor Corporation

Mail Drop Sign

Use this sign on or near the container in which students will place their completed postcards.

Mail Drop

Answer Key

Using Money to Trade

Page 24
1. $8
2. 3 bracelets drawn
3. $14

Page 25
1. 61¢
2. 50¢
3. 11¢

Buying Groceries

Page 36
1. $18
2. no
3. $2

Page 37
1. $2
2. $1
3. $1

Shopping for Clothes

Page 48
1. no; They add up to $43, and she has only $40.
2. $38
3. all but two of the 1-dollar bills should be circled

Page 49
1. $44
2. $15
3. $60

Earning Money in Your Family

Page 60
1. Dust the shelves; Weed the garden
2. $16 in bills and/or coins
3. any combination that adds up to at least $9

Page 61
1. $25
2. the third box should be marked (two 10-dollar bills, four 5-dollar bills)

Saving Money

Page 72
1. $36
2. $40
3. Yes. Explanations will vary but should show that she now has $54 or that she needed $36 and made $40.

Page 73
1. $30
2. $50
3. the fourth box should be marked (2 quarters, 2 dimes, 1 nickel)

Paying at a Restaurant

Page 84
1. $15
2. yes
   Answers will vary but should indicate that 4 quarters equals 1 dollar, and 1 dollar plus 2 dollars equals 3 dollars.

Page 85
1. $30
2. $5
3. $6

Raising Money to Help Others

Page 96
1. $11
2. $48

Page 97
1. $50
2. $6
3. 3

Paying to Go Places

Page 108
1. $100
2. $128

Page 109
1. $16
2. the fourth box should be marked (two 20-dollar bills and three 10-dollar bills)

Using Banks

Paying at the Post Office

FREE Activities
to Help Children Learn!

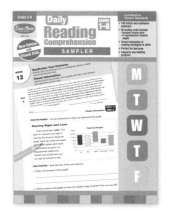

Get **free printable lessons and activities** to use with your students or children.

Scan Me!

https://www.evan-moor.com/free-samplers

FREE Samplers

STEAM

Project-Based Learning

GRADES 1-6

Real-World Learning for Tomorrow's Leaders!

STEAM is an approach to project-based learning that uses **Science, Technology, Engineering, the Arts, and Mathematics** to engage children in empathizing, thinking critically, collaborating, and coming up with solutions to solve real-world problems.

Each robust unit in this classroom resource focuses on a hands-on STEAM project that encourages students to enjoy the journey of creating and sharing his or her solutions to help create a better world.

128 reproducible pages.
Correlated to current standards.

Grade 3

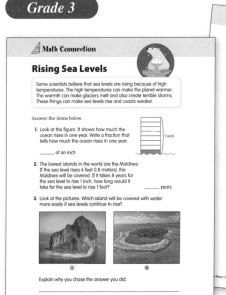

Math Connection

Rising Sea Levels

Some scientists believe that sea levels are rising because of high temperatures. The high temperatures can make the planet warmer. The warmth can make glaciers melt and also create terrible storms. These things can make sea levels rise and coasts weaker.

Answer the items below.

1. Look at the figure. It shows how much the ocean rises in one year. Write a fraction that tells how much the ocean rises in one year.

_____ of an inch

2. The lowest islands in the world are the Maldives. If the sea level rises 6 feet (1.8 meters), the Maldives will be covered. If it takes 8 years for the sea level to rise 1 inch, how long would it take for the sea level to rise 1 foot? _____ years

3. Look at the pictures. Which island will be covered with water more easily if sea levels continue to rise?

Ⓐ   Ⓑ

Explain why you chose the answer you did.

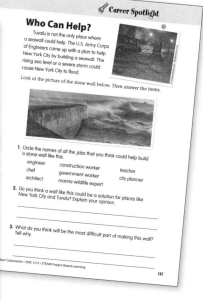

Career Spotlight

Who Can Help?

Tuvalu is not the only place where a seawall could help. The U.S. Army Corps of Engineers came up with a plan to help New York City by building a seawall. The rising sea level or a severe storm could cause New York City to flood.

Look at the picture of the stone wall below. Then answer the items.

1. Circle the names of all the jobs that you think could help build a stone wall like this.

engineer   construction worker   teacher
chef   government worker   city planner
architect   marine wildlife expert

2. Do you think a wall like this could be a solution for places like New York City and Tuvalu? Explain your opinion.

3. What do you think will be the most difficult part of making this wall? Tell why.

Teacher's Edition*

Grade 1	EMC 3111
Grade 2	EMC 3112
Grade 3	EMC 3113
Grade 4	EMC 3114
Grade 5	EMC 3115
Grade 6	EMC 3116

*Available in print and e-book

Weekly

Real-World Writing

Real-World Learning for Tomorrow's Leaders!

Help students explore real-world purposes for writing with activities that demonstrate thoughtful and effective writing strategies.

The **24 writing units** within *Weekly Real-World Writing* focus on six common writing purposes: **self-expression, information, evaluation, inquiry, analysis, and persuasion.**

Weekly activities include letters, journal entries, product opinions, advertisements, directions, interviews, and more!

Units are designed to fit into a weekly lesson plan and include:

- Teacher overview page
- A writing sample to model each skill
- Graphic Organizer for student notes
- Two writing tasks with response pages
- An extension activity

128 reproducible pages.
Correlated to current standards.

Teacher's Resource Book*

Grades 1–2	EMC 6077
Grades 3–4	EMC 6078
Grades 5–6	EMC 6079

*Available in print and e-book

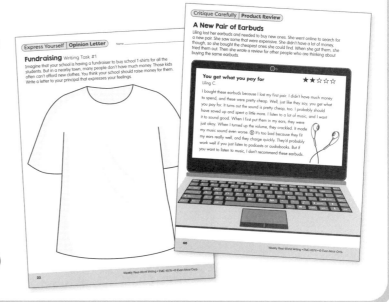

Grade 3

Social and Emotional Learning Activities

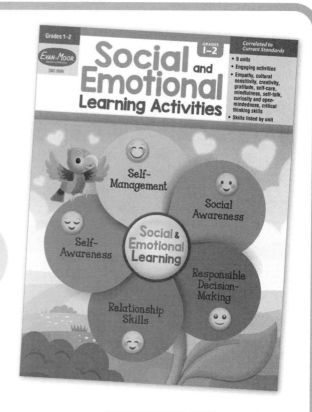

GRADES PreK–6

Real-World Scenarios Give Students Important Life Skills!

Support students by helping them develop, identify, and practice positive behaviors and thoughts with social and emotional learning activities. Research shows that SEL experiences improve student achievement, reduce stress, and increase positive behaviors such as kindness, gratitude, and empathy.

Social and Emotional Learning Activities includes:

- **100+ engaging activities** that weave social and emotional learning activities into the busy school day

- SEL instruction that incorporates **writing, reading, math, social studies,** and **cultural diversity**

- **Creative writing, puzzles, games, art projects,** and **real-world scenarios** that engage children in practicing positive behaviors and boost self-image

The nine units cover the five domains of social and emotional learning:

- Self-Awareness
- Self-Management
- Social Awareness
- Responsible Decision-Making
- Relationship Skills

112 reproducible pages. Correlated to current standards.

Teacher Resource Book*

Grades PreK–K	EMC 6095
Grades 1–2	EMC 6096
Grades 3–4	EMC 6097
Grades 5–6	EMC 6098

Available in print and e-book

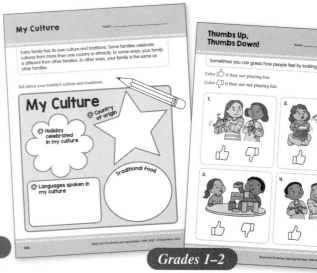

Grades 3–4

Grades 1–2